Also by Thomas M. Stark

Riverhead: The Halcyon Years 1861 to 1919

HORRIFIC HOMICIDES

*A Judge Looks Back at the Amityville Horror Murders
and Other Infamous Long Island Crimes*

THOMAS M. STARK

Archway Publishing books may be ordered through booksellers or by contacting:

Archway Publishing
1663 Liberty Drive
Bloomington, IN 47403
www.archwaypublishing.com
844-669-3957

ISBN: 978-1-6657-1104-3 (sc)
ISBN: 978-1-6657-1105-0 (e)

Library of Congress Control Number: 2021916434

Print information available on the last page.

Archway Publishing rev. date: 10/20/2021

CONTENTS

FOREWORD

Retired New York State Supreme Court Justice Thomas M. Stark died on April 27, 2014, at the age of eighty-nine, soon after finishing this manuscript but before the book could be published. While his daughters have updated the content when possible, some of the information may still reflect where matters stood in 2014. Additions and revisions were based on news reports, Stark's notes, and court filings. Judge Stark left behind unpublished accounts of many more of the trials he presided over during his thirty-seven years on the bench. The stories of three notable ones have been included in the final section of this volume.

—Elizabeth Stark Dugan and Ellen Stark,
June 2021

PREFACE AND ACKNOWLEDGMENTS

I retired in 1998 after serving thirty-seven years as a judge in the New York State Unified Court System. During those years I presided over hundreds of criminal and civil jury and nonjury trials. In thirty-three criminal jury trials the defendant was accused of murder. In four of those cases, the murders collectively caused the deaths of twelve innocent victims, and the trials were high-profile events reported on daily in the Long Island media. This book recounts the details of each of these murders and the police investigations, prosecutions, and legal proceedings that followed.

The most notorious of the murders were those committed by Ronald DeFeo Jr., who used a high-powered hunting rifle to fatally shoot his sleeping parents and four younger siblings in their waterfront home at Amityville, New York, during the early morning hours of November 13, 1974. The site of these killings soon became internationally famous through the pages of *The Amityville Horror: A True Story*, the infamous haunted-house book. The DeFeo family murders generated wide publicity beyond Long Island. The slayings and the arrest of the eldest son were reported on all the wire services, as were his trial and conviction the following year. A number of books have been published about the murders, and several documentary television programs about the crimes, including on-air interviews of the imprisoned DeFeo, have been shown on nationwide cable channels.

One of my most interesting cases was an execution-style murder-for-hire. Frances "Vikki" Ardito enlisted two New York City gunmen to abduct her unfaithful paramour, Benjamin Mattana Jr., from their home in Lloyd Harbor and kill him in a Jamaica Bay marsh early on the morning of April 28, 1976. Ardito went on trial, along with the two gunmen, accused of orchestrating her lover's murder. But during the prosecution's case, her purported mental breakdown led to a mistrial (the two gunmen were convicted). Six years later, after her long hospitalization for her mental illness and its exposure as a fraud, Ardito pled guilty to the kidnapping and murder.

The most horrifying of the murders was committed by East Northport delicatessen owner Anthony Cisco, who importuned his teenaged clerk to throw an army smoke grenade through the front window of a nearby neighbor's house at 1:00 a.m. on May 10, 1980, intending to start a fire and awaken the sleeping occupants. The grenade's detonation quickly filled the house with acrid, suffocating smoke, causing the tragic deaths of the mother and three young children of the sleeping Josefsek family. At the time, the prosecutor called the Josefsek murders "one of the most heinous crimes in Suffolk County history."

The most inexplicable of the murders was committed by off-duty New York City police patrolman Daniel Gallagher, who ended his twenty-four-hour alcohol-fueled celebration of St. Patrick's Day by fatally shooting fellow officer Sergeant Jack Sweeney inside a moving car in Brentwood on the morning of March 18, 1981.

In each of the four murder trials, a different provision of criminal law and procedure was involved. DeFeo, admitting on trial that he shot and killed six family members, raised the insanity defense. His jury had to determine whether his mental state at the time of the killings met the strict requirements of this defense. The Mattana murder trial raised the legal question of Vikki Ardito's mental capacity to continue on trial after her breakdown. Her case also involved the legal proceedings during the six years after her mistrial.

The Cisco murder trial was the most unusual of the four and one of my most interesting cases. Cisco did not intend to cause the death of the four victims when the smoke grenade detonated, but the deaths were legally murders nevertheless, under two other types of murder: felony murder and depraved indifference reckless murder. The Gallagher murder trial presented the legal interaction between intoxication and criminal responsibility in three aspects: the effect of voluntary intoxication, the effect of involuntary intoxication, and the effect of intoxication on reckless conduct.

In writing this book, I relied principally on my recollections. To ensure accuracy and refresh my recollections, I utilized various documents and items: (1) my bench notebooks containing my handwritten notes of each witness's testimony, taken during the four murder trials and related hearings; (2) the transcript of Ronald DeFeo's trial and related hearings prepared by the official court reporter; (3) my retained copies of certain documents, including jury instruction outlines, presentence investigation reports, affidavits, psychiatrist reports, sentencing notes, and judicial hearing decisions; (4) state and federal appellate briefs, appeals court opinions, and state parole board decisions; (5) copies of television documentary programs and published books about the DeFeo family murders; (6) published books about the Amityville Horror hoax; and (7) newspaper articles concerning the murders.

Several individuals helped me obtain public documents and photographs for this publication. Steven Hovani, former chief of the District Attorney Appeals Bureau, arranged for me to examine the official court reporter's transcript of the DeFeo trial and related hearings and the appellate briefs in the state and federal appeals in that case. John L. Buonora, former chief assistant district attorney, obtained from the Suffolk County Police Department archives the arrest photographs (mug shots) of the defendants. He was aided in his efforts by members of the department and District Attorney Appeals Bureau Chief Michael Miller. Their aid is greatly appreciated.

Even though the murders and legal proceedings recounted in this book occurred during the 1970s, 1980s, and 1990s and are now part of Long Island's history, they still graphically demonstrate the horror of the intentional or reckless taking of human lives for immoral and unjustified reasons and how the state deals with such criminal conduct.

PART 1

The Antisocial Son
The DeFeo Family Murders
November 13, 1974

Ronald DeFeo Jr., arrested on November 14, 1974,
for the murders of his parents and siblings

INTRODUCTION

My most notorious criminal case was the 1975 trial of twenty-three-year-old Ronald Joseph DeFeo Jr., who was convicted by a jury of intentionally killing his sleeping parents and four younger siblings in their home in Amityville, Long Island, during the night of November 12–13, 1974. During his lengthy imprisonment, DeFeo recounted various versions of the events of that night in court proceedings and interviews. Those shifting stories include admitting his own guilt in the six murders; denying any guilt whatsoever; blaming others for the six killings; and admitting that he first killed his parents and ultimately his eighteen-year-old sister after she allegedly killed the three younger siblings.

The undisputed fact in this case is that on the morning of November 13, 1974, six bodies lay dead in their beds, each life terminated by bullets fired from Ronald DeFeo's .35-caliber Marlin rifle. The fact that DeFeo was the sole person who fired that rifle into those six family members was established beyond a reasonable doubt to the satisfaction of twelve jurors who examined the evidence presented during a six-week trial and then deliberated for three days. Four experienced appellate judges, after considering the trial record and DeFeo's arguments, came to the same conclusion and upheld his conviction. In the years since the trial, I have never found any basis to question his guilt in the six murders.

The story did not end with DeFeo's guilty verdict. A 1977 best-selling book, *The Amityville Horror: A True Story*, recounted supernatural events allegedly occurring in that Amityville home shortly after the murders. Two years later, a July 27, 1979, *New York Post* headline reported that

the best-selling book was allegedly a hoax: "Lawyer Claims Amityville
Book Was Hokum, not Horror."

Since 1975 I have participated in four videotaped interviews
concerning the DeFeo family murders and the trial, and those interviews
were incorporated into televised documentary programs. The extent of
my broadcast remarks was limited by the time constraints imposed by
television. This horrific crime and its aftermath, the so-called "Amityville
Horror" hoax, deserve a more expanded recounting. This narrative tells
the entire story that produced the headlines and the best seller.

A GRUESOME DISCOVERY

A November 14, 1974, *New York Times* front-page headline reported
the discovery of a horrific crime in Amityville, New York: "Six
in Family Found Slain in Bedrooms in L.I. Home." The front
page of the *Daily News* screamed, "Find 6 in Family Shot to Death."
The bodies had been discovered the previous evening after a friend of
Ronald "Butch" DeFeo called the police. As New Yorkers read about the
crime, the first of DeFeo's many versions of what had transpired in his
Amityville home was already coming out.

In 1974, Amityville was a compact village of ten thousand situated
on the north shore of Great South Bay at the western edge of Suffolk
County. The DeFeo residence fronted on Amityville Creek, an inlet that
led to the bay. The house on 112 Ocean Avenue—which was named
"High Hopes"—was a three-story Dutch colonial that stood sideways
on a narrow lot, with a patio, swimming pool, and a garage/boathouse
in the rear. A one-car driveway ran between the house and the adjoining
property to the south. A statue of St. Joseph holding the baby Jesus stood
in the yard.

The house was built in the 1920s and had been owned and occupied
by the DeFeo family since 1965. It had three bedrooms, a television

room, and two baths on the second floor; two bedrooms and a bath on the third floor; a living room, dining room, enclosed sun porch, and kitchen on the main floor; and a furnished basement.

Ronald DeFeo Sr., forty-three, and his wife, Louise Brigante DeFeo, forty-two, occupied the master bedroom on the second floor. Down the hall were Allison DeFeo, thirteen, who had her own bedroom, and Marc DeFeo, twelve, and John DeFeo, nine, who shared a bedroom. Ronald DeFeo Jr., twenty-three, and Dawn DeFeo, eighteen, each occupied a third-floor bedroom. Ronald DeFeo Sr. was employed as service manager at Brigante-Karl Buick, 800 Coney Island Avenue in Brooklyn. His father-in-law, Michael Brigante Sr., was the owner of this large automobile dealership, and Ronald DeFeo Jr. worked there as an assistant in the service department. Louise DeFeo was the only daughter of Brigante, and he always made sure that his daughter's family had no financial concerns. He provided the money for the purchase of the Amityville house and doted on his five grandchildren. Neighbors described the family as close knit—a "nice, normal family," a *New York Times* headline would later say.

That world was turned upside down in November 1974. At a pretrial hearing ten months later, police officers testified that Ronald DeFeo Jr. told them that shortly after six o'clock on the evening of November 13, 1974, he left Henry's Bar in Amityville and drove home, where he found his father and mother lying in their bed, dead of gunshot wounds. Returning to the bar in a hysterical state, he told his friends that his parents had been shot. He and five others drove back to his home, and one friend, Robert "Bobby" Kelske, looked at the bodies and asked DeFeo what to do. Call the police and his grandparents, he told Kelske.

Amityville police officer Kenneth Greguski responded to the call at 6:35 p.m., entered the house, went upstairs, saw the parents' bodies and the bodies of Marc and John DeFeo in their beds, and called his headquarters. Reporting that he'd found four bodies, he requested that Suffolk County Police be notified. DeFeo, who was upset and crying, overheard the call and told Greguski that he also had two sisters. Returning upstairs, Greguski found the bodies of Allison and Dawn

DeFeo in their beds and called headquarters again, now reporting finding a total of six bodies, all clad in nightclothes and none showing any sign of struggle.

Suffolk County Police Homicide Squad officers arrived, and a detective asked DeFeo whether he knew who could have done it. DeFeo mentioned a man named Tony Mazzeo. After police made arrangements to use an adjoining house as crime scene headquarters, DeFeo was further questioned there. He again said the murders might have been committed by Mazzeo, and detectives began to write down what DeFeo was telling them.

By about 8:00 p.m. a large crowd of people—including reporters, neighbors, and onlookers—was congregating at the scene. A priest had come by to offer prayers. So the police decided to continue DeFeo's questioning at First Squad headquarters in North Lindenhurst. Once there, DeFeo told detectives that he wanted to help their investigation, and he recounted in detail his activities on the previous day, November 12, and the present day, November 13.

He explained to detectives that he had stayed home from work on November 12 because of stomach trouble and watched television that night. He fell asleep, still sitting in the second-floor television room, and woke up about four o'clock in the morning, at which point he decided to go to work early, driving by himself because his father was staying home that day. He described traveling to Brooklyn, eating an early breakfast at a Coney Island diner, and arriving at the Buick dealer service department before 7:00 a.m. Because he was on probation for having a stolen outboard motor a year earlier, he said he called home several times to ask his family to leave out his pay stubs to show his probation officer, but no one answered the phone. After leaving work in the early afternoon, he drove to Amityville, met his girlfriend, Mindy Weiss, and went with her to the mall in nearby Massapequa. Then he visited a friend's house, where he said he shot heroin, and ended up at Henry's Bar in the late afternoon, joining other friends.

DeFeo told the police more about the man he suspected, Tony Mazzeo, giving considerable details about incidents between Mazzeo

　　THOMAS M. STARK

and his father that supported his suspicions. Mazzeo had been a friend of his father's, he said, though that friendship had soured. Before then Mazzeo and his wife had temporarily lived with the family in Amityville. Mazzeo, who still had a key to the house, was one of the few people who knew that Ronald Sr. had hidden cash under a doorsill in the master bedroom, DeFeo said.

He also claimed Mazzeo was connected to organized crime figures (referring to him as a "professional murderer") and that his great-uncle, Peter DeFeo, was mob-connected too. DeFeo's suspicions about possible organized crime involvement in the murders were immediately conveyed to the Suffolk County Police Department Organized Crime Section, whose officers began a wide-reaching investigation of organized crime sources on Long Island and Manhattan.

By late evening, the detectives had written down what DeFeo had told them in an eight-page statement. DeFeo read and signed the statement, swearing to its truth. Because of his remarks about organized crime involvement, the detectives drove DeFeo to Fourth Squad headquarters in Hauppauge for further questioning. He told the police that because he was the sole surviving family member, he was fearful of Mazzeo and wanted to stick close to the police in a secure place. At Hauppauge, DeFeo was questioned further and, when asked about any weapons in the house, said that his father had taken his guns from him some time ago.

DeFeo was becoming tired and wanted to sleep but said he was fearful of being brought to his DeFeo relatives in West Islip. Accordingly, the detectives set up a cot in the nearby homicide squad headquarters, and DeFeo, after having a sandwich and a drink, fell asleep. During the evening of November 13 and the early morning hours of November 14, the investigating detectives did not suspect that DeFeo was involved in the murders. His demeanor and statements pointed to the crimes having been committed by others, and police efforts were directed to questioning other DeFeo family members, neighbors, and friends, as well as investigating possible organized crime involvement.

DeFeo's written statement differed from that of a suspect, which would have included the required Miranda advice and waivers. The statements appeared plausible to the detectives, and they testified that they had no extrinsic evidence implicating him in the crimes.

A NEW SUSPECT EMERGES

After 3:00 a.m. on November 14, while DeFeo was sleeping, the detectives received information indicating his possible involvement in the crimes. The Police Laboratory reported that the expended bullets found in the DeFeo house were fired from a .35-caliber Marlin rifle. Kelske had told the police that DeFeo was a "gun buff," very familiar with guns, and that one of his guns was a .35-caliber Marlin. He'd also told them that DeFeo had gotten his guns back from his father and had been attempting to buy a silencer. The Homicide Squad detectives conferred, and DeFeo became a definite suspect in the murders. (Later that morning police searched DeFeo's bedroom in Amityville and found his other weapons: a .22-caliber semiautomatic rifle, a 12-gauge shotgun, a .22-caliber blank revolver, .22-caliber cartridges, and 12-gauge shotgun shells—confirmation that he was a gun enthusiast.)

DeFeo slept until 9:00 a.m., when he was awakened by the detectives and told that he was the man they were looking for. It was no longer Mazzeo. Now a suspect, DeFeo was read the required Miranda rights. DeFeo said he understood his right to remain silent and that anything he did say could be used against him, and he agreed to waive these rights. When told of his right to consult a lawyer and to have a lawyer provided if necessary, he said he didn't need a lawyer and was willing to talk without one. He continued to insist that Mazzeo committed the murders. DeFeo was then given breakfast.

The detectives told DeFeo that the bullets were fired from a .35-caliber Marlin rifle and that they knew he owned such a gun. They even showed him the Marlin rifle carton that had been found in his bedroom. While DeFeo still wasn't admitting to the murders, he started to speak harshly about his parents, siblings, and grandfather, exhibiting great animosity toward them all.

In the meantime, Detective Dennis Rafferty, an experienced homicide interrogator, and Lieutenant Robert Dunn, commanding officer of the Organized Crime Section, were brought up-to-date on the status of the investigation. At 10:30 a.m., they took over the questioning of DeFeo.

Rafferty and Dunn first questioned DeFeo about his activities during the two previous days, and he repeated the statements he had made the night before. Over the next several hours, DeFeo gradually changed his story, conceding that the killings must have taken place before he left the house. When told he must have heard something, he first admitted to hearing two gunshots before leaving the house, then said he'd heard seven gunshots coming from different bedrooms. Pressed for details, he added that he'd heard footsteps on the second floor. DeFeo drew a diagram of the bedroom locations and who occupied them for these two officers, who were not familiar with the house.

After further questioning, DeFeo admitted seeing his parents' dead bodies. Eventually he admitted he'd seen all six bodies in their beds and the empty cartridge cases nearby. He also told Rafferty and Dunn that he had found his Marlin rifle in Dawn's bedroom. At that point, he had collected the cartridge cases from the bedrooms and put them into an empty pillowcase along with a rifle scabbard, a leather holster, .35-caliber rifle ammunition, and the clothing he was wearing (blue jeans, a work shirt, socks, and undershorts). His clothing was bloodstained, he said, from picking up the cartridge case lying in a pool of blood in Allison's room. He showered and dressed in fresh clothing, putting the damp towel into the pillowcase as well, and left the house.

After throwing the rifle into the water down the street, DeFeo told detectives, he drove to Brooklyn and left the filled pillowcase in a storm drain. DeFeo drew a diagram outlining his route to the storm drain. Other detectives were brought into the room, and DeFeo drew another diagram showing a more detailed location of the storm drain, as well as one showing the dock where he threw the rifle into the water.

Pressed for more about the murders, DeFeo said Mazzeo and another man had entered the house armed and forced him to shoot his parents and one brother with the Marlin rifle, and that Mazzeo took the rifle and shot the others. Rafferty told DeFeo this account was incredible and suggested that he alone had done the shooting. DeFeo began to cry and said, "I just started, and it went so fast I couldn't stop." Dunn said he was awed by the immensity and horror of this admission and left the room, while Rafferty and Detective George Harrison remained.

Rafferty asked DeFeo to give more details of the killings, and DeFeo told this story: After awakening in the television room about 3:00 a.m., he went up to his bedroom, loaded his Marlin rifle with seven cartridges and went down to the second floor. Standing just inside the door of the master bedroom where his parents were sleeping, he fired two shots into his father's back, then shifted his aim to his mother and fired two shots into her chest. He crossed the hall to the door of Allison's bedroom and fired one shot into her head as she turned toward him in her bed. Moving into his brothers' adjoining bedroom and standing at the foot of their twin beds, he fired one shot into each brother's back. He then went up to his bedroom, partially reloaded the rifle and went into his sister Dawn's adjoining bedroom, where he found her standing. Pushing her back into bed, he fired one shot into her head.

DeFeo also repeated his account of collecting the empty cartridge cases, changing his clothing, taking the filled pillowcase and the rifle with him, and disposing of them. Asked if he would sign a written statement containing these admissions, he said he would not because he feared his grandfather, Michael Brigante, would see it. The November 14 interrogation was briefly interrupted in early afternoon when food and drink for the detectives and DeFeo was sent into the interview room.

All of the detectives who questioned DeFeo during the day of November 14 testified that during this period DeFeo never asked to leave the interview room, to make any telephone calls, or to contact an attorney. They testified that no police officer used or threatened the use of physical force or used any improper means to obtain DeFeo's incriminatory statements, and that his statements were entirely voluntary.

The detectives who went to Brooklyn, using the two diagrams drawn by DeFeo, found the storm drain and removed the filled pillowcase. On their return to Hauppauge, they delivered the empty cartridge cases to the police laboratory. They brought the clothing and other items to homicide squad headquarters, where DeFeo was now seated in the squad room. Shown the clothing and other items, DeFeo admitted they were his and initialed them. He also told the detectives who had recovered the pillowcase that he had admitted the killings to the interrogating detectives. The clothing DeFeo was wearing was taken. Arrested the evening of November 14, he was lodged in detention for the night.

The next day, police divers searched the water off the Amityville dock where DeFeo had thrown the Marlin rifle and recovered it. He was indicted by the grand jury on November 18, accused of six counts of intentional murder by shooting each of his family members with a rifle. On the same day, at St. Martin of Tours Roman Catholic Church in Amityville, six members of his family were laid to rest at a funeral mass attended by nearly a thousand friends, family, and neighbors.

A MURDER TRIAL ASSIGNED

On September 17, 1975, I was contacted by the assignment judge of the County Court, who advised me that a murder trial pending in that court had been transferred by the county administrative judge to the Criminal Term of the Supreme Court, where I was presiding. The murder trial was that of Ronald Joseph DeFeo Jr., who was accused of killing six members of his own family at their home in Amityville, Long Island, during the early morning hours of November 13, 1974.

Along with the populace of Suffolk County, I was already familiar with this case. When the murders were discovered, the fact that an entire family of father, mother, and four children had been found dead in their beds of gunshot wounds was the leading story on that night's local television and radio news broadcasts and in the area newspapers the following morning. After the eldest DeFeo son was arrested on the afternoon of November 14, 1974, and charged with the killings, the case became even more newsworthy.

After his arrest, DeFeo had been arraigned in the district court and remanded to the county jail at Riverhead without bail. His grandfather Michael Brigante retained prominent defense attorney Jacob Siegfried to represent his grandson. A psychiatric examination by two doctors found DeFeo mentally competent to understand the charges and assist in his defense. The district attorney provided Siegfried with the particulars of the charges: when the killings had taken place on the morning of November 13, 1974 (between two o'clock and four o'clock), the weapon used—a .35-caliber Marlin lever-action rifle—and where the bodies were found. Siegfried was provided with a copy of DeFeo's written statement to the police, the substance of his oral statements, and copies of the six autopsy reports on the victims' bodies.

On March 11, 1975, a County Court judge found the evidence presented to the grand jury legally sufficient and directed a pretrial suppression hearing be conducted. The purpose was to determine whether DeFeo's oral and written statements given to the police during their investigation and the evidence found as a result of his statements were admissible on trial. On May 15, Siegfried filed a notice that DeFeo intended to raise the insanity defense at trial and would also raise the defense that he acted under the influence of extreme emotional disturbance.

A few weeks later, on May 27, Siegfried withdrew as DeFeo's counsel. He told the court that he and his client had serious disagreements concerning trial strategy and that DeFeo had threatened him physically. During the next several weeks, DeFeo insisted that he be allowed to select his own new attorney. Brigante did not approve and chose not to pay a new attorney's fees. Under these circumstances, in that DeFeo had no funds of his own, on July 7, 1975, Judge Ernest Signorelli of the County Court appointed an attorney whose compensation would be paid from public funds. He selected William E. Weber from the list of qualified attorneys maintained by the administrator of the assigned counsel plan. Weber, thirty-five, a graduate of Brooklyn Law School, was a member of the law firm of Mars and Burton of Patchogue, Long Island. He practiced as a criminal and civil trial lawyer.

The assistant district attorney assigned to prosecute the case was Gerard B. Sullivan, deputy chief of the District Attorney's trial bureau. Sullivan, thirty-three, a graduate of St. John's University Law School, was an experienced felony prosecutor who had spent his entire career in the district attorney's office. Weber moved quickly to complete the pretrial proceedings. The judge allowed Weber to hire a private investigator and two psychiatrists and to order transcripts of all court proceedings, all at public expense. Weber hired an investigator and made arrangements for DeFeo's psychiatric examination in preparation for the insanity defense.

Years later, Sullivan co-wrote an excellent book about the DeFeo case, entitled *High Hopes: The Amityville Murders*. Upon reading it, I found out for the first time how the trial ended up in my court after a bit of "judge shopping" by the district attorney. Knowing that Weber was a "bulldog" in the courtroom, Sullivan wrote, and anticipating clashes, he said he wanted a judge who couldn't be pushed around, "The only judge in Suffolk County who possessed that kind of total control was Thomas M. Stark, a hawk-nosed, hazel-eyed, Harvard Law graduate … [with] the rare ability to immobilize an obstreperous attorney with a single stare over the silver-framed half-glasses he wore halfway down his nose."

When the DeFeo trial was transferred to me, I scheduled a hearing right away. At the time I was using a small courtroom in the Griffing Avenue Court Complex in Riverhead. This courtroom was not equipped to accommodate a criminal trial where the defendant was in custody. Accordingly, I moved to a vacant courtroom in the new criminal court building located adjacent to the jail. This courthouse had separate interior corridors leading from the prisoner receiving area to each courtroom and holding cells adjoining the courtrooms. Thus, DeFeo, when brought

THE STATEMENTS STAND

from jail to court each day, did not have to be moved within the public areas of the building.

On September 22, 1975, a nonjury hearing began before me and went on for six days. Under New York law, any oral or written statement made by a suspect cannot be used as evidence upon trial unless it was voluntarily made. DeFeo claimed that the written and oral statements he made before his arrest were involuntary—that the police had severely beaten him and denied him access to his attorney while holding him against his will. He asked me to order that his statements and the evidence found as a result of these statements be suppressed—that is, they could not be used by the district attorney on trial.

Even though DeFeo was required to present evidence supporting his claims in the hearing, the district attorney had the ultimate burden of proving to me beyond a reasonable doubt that DeFeo's statements were voluntary. Sullivan was assisted by a young assistant district attorney, Thomas J. Spota, who remained on the case during the entire trial. (After the DeFeo case was concluded, Spota continued as a career felony prosecutor and was elected Suffolk County district attorney four times before being forced to resign amid charges that he helped cover up a police beating of a suspect.)

Twenty witnesses, including DeFeo, testified at the hearing. Seventeen items were put in evidence as exhibits. First up was the district attorney's evidence concerning the police investigation and questioning of DeFeo during the evening of November 13 and November 14. Weber then presented DeFeo's evidence. His first witness was Kelske, who testified that he was questioned by the police throughout the evening of November 13 and into the morning hours of November 14 and gave them a written statement containing his knowledge of the DeFeo family and the events of November 13. At the time, he believed the police considered him an accomplice in the shootings. Kelske said that he told the police about DeFeo's ownership of guns, including the Marlin rifle, and his shooting ability.

Michael Brigante Sr., DeFeo's maternal grandfather, testified that he, his wife, and his son came from Brooklyn after learning of the murders, but that the police forbade him from entering his daughter's home during the evening's investigation. He remained, grief-stricken, outside the house with his wife, son, and Richard Wyssling, his nephew by marriage, who had also come to the house. When he asked a detective where his grandson Ronald DeFeo Jr. was, Brigante said he was told that he was at the First Precinct headquarters (the same building where First Squad headquarters is located). Wanting his grandson to be with the family, Brigante asked Wyssling to find him.

At the hearing, Wyssling testified that he had approached Brigante and told him that DeFeo should be represented by an attorney, and that he, being an attorney, could protect DeFeo's rights. Wyssling said he informed a detective at the crime scene that he was representing DeFeo and was informed that DeFeo was at the First Precinct headquarters. Driving there, he told the desk officer that he represented DeFeo, who he understood had been charged with six counts of murder, and that he didn't want him questioned. Told that DeFeo was at the Fourth Precinct headquarters (the same building where Fourth Squad headquarters was located), Wyssling drove there and said that he advised the desk officer that he was DeFeo's attorney and asked that any questioning of him be stopped. Upon being told that DeFeo was not there, he left the precinct and returned to the house, telling Brigante he was unable to locate his grandson. Brigante, along with his wife and son, returned to Brooklyn at about midnight.

DeFeo was Weber's final witness. Testifying as to his activities during the day of November 13, he largely repeated what was in his eight-page written statement. He denied having read the statement but reiterated his suspicions that Mazzeo was the murderer. According to the version of his story he told on the stand during the hearing, he had objected to being taken by the police to the First Squad headquarters. He'd wanted to remain at the crime scene but was forced to leave. Despite his repeated requests to contact the attorney who had represented him on the stolen property conviction, the police refused. He also asked to contact his family, and this was also refused. DeFeo denied being given any food or drink or being allowed to sleep at homicide squad headquarters, and said he signed the written statement only when told he could go home if he did so. At 9:00 a.m. on November 14, he was informed that the police now had evidence that he killed his family, according to his testimony, and after that three other detectives entered the room and viciously beat him, hitting him in the face, punching him in the stomach, kicking him in the back, and stomping upon him.

After this beating, DeFeo said, Detective Rafferty and Lieutenant Dunn entered the room, the others left, and he was handcuffed to a cabinet while being questioned. He testified that he answered yes to whatever they told him about the killings, never admitted shooting his family, and didn't tell the police about the disposal of the items in the Brooklyn storm drain or its location.

Sullivan then presented evidence in rebuttal. The attorney who represented DeFeo at his arraignment in the district court on November 15 testified that DeFeo had a small cut above his left eyebrow, which was not open or bleeding, and that his lips appeared to be swollen. To show how this cut occurred, John Donahue, a schoolmate and friend of nine-year-old John DeFeo, was called to testify. He said he was visiting John at the DeFeo home in the late afternoon two days before the murders. While he and John were playing pool in the basement, Ronald DeFeo Jr. and his father came down and asked the two boys to go upstairs. However, they only went to the top of the steps and from there watched DeFeo and his father get into an altercation, with DeFeo punching his father, who punched him back in the face.

Patrolman Thomas Muratore testified that he was on duty at the front desk of the Fourth Precinct headquarters on the night of November 13 when Richard Wyssling came in about midnight, asked if Ronald DeFeo Jr. was there, and said he was a friend of the family. Muratore

     THOMAS M. STARK

checked the uniformed officers and detectives squad rooms, was told no such person was there, and reported this to Wyssling. He denied Wyssling saying anything about being a lawyer. Having no knowledge of the DeFeo family murders when he came on duty the previous evening, the name meant nothing to him at the time. Later, in the building lobby, Muratore saw Wyssling talking to Lieutenant David Menzies.

Lieutenant Menzies, squad commander of the Fourth Precinct, testified that he was on duty at precinct headquarters the night of November 13 and learned of the ongoing investigation of the murders, and that DeFeo was then present in the detectives' area of precinct headquarters. At about 1:00 a.m. on November 14, he was called to the front desk, where Wyssling was waiting. Wyssling identified himself as an attorney but said he did not represent DeFeo, that he was there as a friend of the family and wanted to see DeFeo. Menzies said he told Wyssling that the detectives were talking to DeFeo and that he should contact homicide later.

In court, after the completion of the hearing testimony, both attorneys made closing arguments to me and filed written memoranda of the law concerning the interrogation of suspects. Three issues of fact required my determination:

1. Were DeFeo's oral admissions of murdering his family the result of police brutality and therefore involuntary?
2. Was the physical evidence found by the police a result of DeFeo's involuntary oral statements and diagrams?
3. Did the police deny DeFeo's constitutionally guaranteed access to an attorney prior to or during his interrogation and therefore render his statements involuntary?

I decided these issues by judging the credibility of each witness's testimony. Was the testimony truthful or untruthful? This required me to consider many factors: Was a witness's testimony corroborated by other evidence? Were there consistencies or inconsistencies in a witness's testimony? Did a witness have a motive to testify falsely? Did a witness have a bias or hostility for or against the prosecution or defendant? Was a witness's testimony reasonable or unreasonable? I also considered the witness's manner or bearing while testifying and the witness's ability to recall events and conversations.

After these evaluations and credibility judgments, I found that the majority of the hearing witnesses gave truthful testimony. However, I found that the testimony of Wyssling as to his conversations with Brigante at the crime scene and with various police officers at the crime scene and the First and Fourth Precinct headquarters was untruthful. His bias against the prosecution clearly showed during his testimony. At the time he was awaiting trial on a grand jury indictment for perjury, and when questioned about this charge he showed an attitude of vindictiveness against the district attorney's office. This bias, in my opinion, was the reason for his attempt to deliberately weaken the prosecution's case. He also had the sequence of the investigation mixed up when he testified that he told the First Precinct desk officer on the evening of November 13 that DeFeo was "charged with six counts of murder." In fact, at that time DeFeo was not a suspect, and it was seventeen hours later when he confessed and was charged. For these and other reasons, Wyssling's testimony was, in my opinion, unconvincing.

I also found that DeFeo's testimony was largely untruthful. As the accused murderer, DeFeo was what the law calls an interested witness, that is, he had a vital interest in the outcome of the case. DeFeo's interest in wanting to keep his incriminatory admissions and other evidence out of the case was one factor I considered in finding his testimony untruthful. His testimony that he was given no food or drink, nor permitted to sleep for over twenty-four hours, was totally unreasonable and unbelievable. His failure to complain to the district court judge on November 15 about the alleged extreme police brutality the previous day, nor to mention it in any documents supporting his pretrial motions, was a factor leading me to believe it never occurred.

His denial that he told the police the location of the obscure Brooklyn storm drain where he secreted the evidence, when, in fact, they found the items within hours using his diagrams, was so flagrant a falsehood as to raise suspicion of the truthfulness of the balance of his testimony.

His inability to even describe the three detectives who allegedly beat him was another factor I considered in finding his testimony to be false.

Overall, I found beyond a reasonable doubt that DeFeo's oral and written statements and diagrams were voluntarily made under New York law and therefore admissible on trial. I also found that he was not denied access to an attorney by the police. Up until 3:00 a.m. on November 14, DeFeo's statements appeared reasonable and plausible, and police had no evidence linking him to the crime. His written statement from the evening of November 13 was a witness statement, not that of a suspect.

On October 1, 1975, I read my lengthy handwritten decision into the court record. The courtroom was nearly filled, including interested assistant district attorneys, the principal homicide squad detectives who had worked on the case, and court buffs. The hearing itself had been lightly attended, since no potential witness was allowed in the courtroom while other witnesses were testifying, a caution to ensure a potential witness does not tailor his testimony to exactly agree with earlier witnesses.

DeFeo exhibited no discernible reaction to my decision, and Weber noted the customary "exception" to ensure my decision could be reviewed on appeal if DeFeo were ultimately convicted. I then directed that jury selection begin on October 6. Weber sought an adjournment of the trial to investigate whether another person was an accomplice of DeFeo in the commission of the murders. I ruled that even if there was an accomplice, DeFeo still could be tried alone as an accessory, and I adhered to my trial date. The following day Weber appealed my refusal to delay the trial and asked the Appellate Division of the Supreme Court in Brooklyn to stay the trial for thirty days to give him additional time to prepare. Four days later the requested stay was denied. The trial could proceed.

THE PEOPLE V. RONALD J. DEFEO JR.

The trial commenced on Monday, October 6, 1975, with jury selection. That day was the opening of the October term of the courts, and about 600 people were coming to Riverhead for jury service. I asked the commissioner of jurors to separate 120 people upon their arrival and keep them apart from the others. There had been considerable publicity about the pretrial hearing and the upcoming trial, and I wanted to minimize gossip about the DeFeo trial among those reporting to Riverhead that morning.

I moved to a larger courtroom for jury selection. This courtroom had many more spectator seats and could accommodate the 120 prospective jurors. Before the prospective jurors entered the courtroom, DeFeo was already seated at the counsel table with Weber. DeFeo was a husky man, five feet, eight inches, 175 pounds. When arrested he was bearded with a mustache, sideburns, and collar-length hair. At the trial he was clean-shaven with only a small mustache and shorter hair. He was dressed in the same outfit he was to wear during the entire trial: light brown plaid jacket, dark green slacks, and a yellow shirt (unbuttoned over his upper chest) with no tie.

As I entered the courtroom, with the prospective jurors present, the clerk announced the name of the case on trial: "The People of the State of New York against Ronald Joseph DeFeo Jr." There was an audible gasp from a prospective juror—"Jesus Christ, it's the DeFeo trial"—head shaking within the group, and the sound of murmuring. Obviously, some recalled reading about the sensational murders nearly eleven months earlier.

I introduced assistant district attorney Sullivan and defense attorney Weber and explained their respective functions and responsibilities during a criminal trial. Sullivan was square-built, Irish-looking, extroverted, with an ego for trial work. He had a commanding voice and was aggressive in the courtroom. Weber was a bright lawyer, pugnacious, tended to dominate the courtroom, and was argumentative with judges. Both lawyers were well acquainted with the rules of evidence and quick to object during their opponent's questioning of witnesses when they perceived an error.

My introduction of DeFeo was simply to point him out and explain that he was the defendant, that is, the person accused of having committed the crimes. I explained that he had no burden or responsibility of proving anything during trial. It was the district attorney who had the burden of proving the defendant's guilt beyond a reasonable doubt. I briefly explained the murder charges contained in the indictment and emphasized that the indictment was simply an accusation and not proof of anything. (Often the function of an indictment is misunderstood by some members of the public, who consider it proof of guilt.) I told the prospective jurors that the trial would be lengthy, probably six to seven weeks, and asked any who could not serve that long to explain their reason. Thirty-two were excused after stating valid reasons.

Twelve names were then drawn at random and these persons seated in the jury box. I questioned them initially as to their qualifications, followed by Sullivan and Weber. Challenges were then exercised, either for a particular cause or peremptorily (each side is allowed a specific number of peremptory challenges for which no reason has to be given), and the resulting empty seats were then filled by random drawing. The selection process continued for four days until a jury of six men and six women satisfactory to both sides was chosen, along with four alternate jurors who could be used if one or more of the regular jurors had to be excused during trial (one alternate was ultimately substituted in midtrial). The twelve jury members came from various Suffolk County communities and included two Grumman Aircraft employees, one Sperry Gyroscope employee, one Consolidated Edison employee, one *Long Island Press* (daily newspaper) employee, one retired mechanic, one supermarket employee, two businessmen, and three housewives.

After opening statements by both attorneys, the district attorney's evidence was presented through the testimony of twenty witnesses (another thirteen would testify in rebuttal of the defense case) and 139 trial exhibits, which included crime-scene photos, the Marlin rifle, and sketches DeFeo drew to show police the location of the Brooklyn storm drain where he'd dumped evidence. The first witness was Amityville Police Officer Kenneth Greguski, the initial officer to respond to the DeFeo house. His testimony introduced the jury to the extensive police investigation of the crime scene.

Dr. Howard Adelman, a forensic pathologist and deputy medical examiner of Suffolk County, testified as to his examination of the victims' bodies in their beds at the house on the evening of November 13 and his autopsy of each body at the morgue. He described each bullet wound, the internal bullet track, and the organs penetrated. He believed that Ronald DeFeo Sr. could have remained alive after the first shot to his back and moved in the bed before the second shot, which was fatal. Adelman testified that Louise DeFeo was awakened by the first shot to her husband and rose part way in the bed before being shot twice in the chest. Allison DeFeo had awakened but died instantly after being shot once in the head, Adelman said, and both Marc and John DeFeo died instantly after receiving one shot each in the back. Dawn DeFeo had awakened in her third-floor bedroom and gotten up from bed before dying instantly from one shot to the head. Adelman testified that all of the victims had been shot at very close range, with the muzzle of the rifle only a few feet from their bodies when fired.

In his opinion, the deaths of Ronald DeFeo Sr., Louise DeFeo, Marc DeFeo, and John DeFeo were caused by massive internal and external hemorrhage after penetration of various organs, while the deaths of Allison DeFeo and Dawn DeFeo were caused by external hemorrhage of head and brain. John's spinal cord was severed by the bullet, and this caused reflex movement of the feet and toes after the shot. DeFeo had told Detectives Rafferty and Harrison that John's feet were "twitching" after he shot him, and Adelman's testimony was elicited to show that DeFeo, to have seen this reflex movement, was in the room when John was shot. DeFeo had told the psychiatrists who examined him for the insanity defense that he was not in the bedroom when John was shot.

During Adelman's testimony, graphic color photographs of each victim as they lay dead in their beds, showing their bloody wounds, were circulated among the jurors. Overall, the testimony of the medical examiner and the photographs showed the jury the horror of the six murders and set the stage for the police testimony that followed.

Next, the homicide squad officers who had investigated the crime scene, recovered physical evidence, and interrogated DeFeo testified. Detective Rafferty, Lieutenant Dunn, and Detective Harrison told the jury of DeFeo's November 14 oral statements, in which he described how he shot and killed all six members of his family, and his description of his activities after the murders: collecting the empty cartridge cases, showering, dressing in fresh clothing, throwing the rifle into the water, leaving the pillowcase containing the cartridge cases and his blood-stained clothing in a Brooklyn storm drain, going to work at Brigante-Karl Buick, returning to Amityville, visiting his girlfriend and his friend, Robert Kelske, and ending up at Henry's Bar. A Nassau County police diver described searching for and recovering the Marlin rifle off the dock at the end of Ocean Avenue.

Detective/Sergeant Alfred Della Penna, chief of the firearms identification section of the Suffolk County police laboratory, was an important witness for the district attorney. A highly qualified ballistics expert, he came to the crime scene the evening of November 13. He searched the area near each body and recovered five intact expended bullets that had passed through five of the bodies. Returning to the laboratory, he examined these bullets and determined from the distinctive pattern of the rifling that each had been fired from a .35-caliber Marlin rifle and provided this information immediately to the investigating homicide squad detectives.

While testifying, he held the Marlin rifle, which was now in evidence, and demonstrated to the jury how it operated. When fully loaded it held seven cartridges, and after each shot the lever action caused the empty cartridge case to be ejected to the right in a rear direction as a new live cartridge was moved into the chamber for the next shot. Intact bullets had been found in the bodies of Ronald DeFeo Sr. and Louise

DeFeo during their autopsies and sent to the laboratory for examination. The eight empty cartridge cases found in the Brooklyn storm drain were also sent the laboratory.

Having the expended bullets, the cartridge cases, and the Marlin rifle, Della Penna was able to determine whether the bullets and the cartridge cases had been fired from that particular rifle. To determine that, he test-fired the rifle in an indoor police range, using the same type .35-caliber ammunition, and recovered the expended bullet. By comparing the test-fired bullet with each expended bullet found at the crime scene and at the autopsies, he determined that the expended bullets from Ronald Sr., Louise, Marc, John, and Dawn DeFeo had been fired from this rifle. The second bullet from Louise and the bullet from Allison DeFeo had insufficient markings to show a match. He also compared the marks left from the firing pin on the base of each empty cartridge case with the marks on the test-fired cartridge case and determined that all the recovered empty cartridges cases had been fired from this rifle. To present the results of these ballistic tests to the jury, Della Penna displayed enlarged photographs of the comparisons. Overall, his expert testimony conclusively showed the jury that each of the six victims had been killed by bullets fired from DeFeo's Marlin rifle.

DeFeo had told Detective Rafferty that the family sheepdog was "howling" while he committed the murders. The prosecution presented a young neighbor, John Nemeth, who said he was awakened by a nearby dog barking at about 3:00 a.m. and recognized it as the DeFeo's. Nemeth, fourteen, who lived two doors away on Ocean Avenue, got up when he heard the dog, went to the window and believed the dog was outside the DeFeo house. He said the noise continued for about twenty minutes. During their investigation, the police found dog hairs and scratch marks inside a garbage can shed on the north side of the DeFeo house, which faced the Nemeth house. Detective Nicholas Severino of the police laboratory compared hairs from the DeFeo sheepdog with those from the shed and testified that they matched.

A waitress, Deborah Cosentino, was driving home from work between 3:30 a.m. and 3:45 a.m., and she testified that as she passed the DeFeo house she noticed that the inside lights on the upper floors were on. Through these three witnesses, the district attorney established the time of the crimes as being between 3:00 a.m. and 4:00 a.m. on November 13.

Phyllis DeFeo Procita, sister of Ronald DeFeo Sr., testified. She had visited her nephew monthly at the jail before the trial, and during these visits she asked him about the murders. He never admitted to her that he was involved, but he began telling her different versions of what occurred. On one occasion he told her that he hid in the crawl space near his bedroom after being awakened by gunshots and heard children screaming, then went down to the second floor, looked at the victims, and found the telephones dead.

On another visit she said he claimed that Bobby Kelske came over and got high on drugs with him in the television room. Kelske fell asleep, and DeFeo left the house after telling Dawn to wake Kelske in the morning. When he returned later, he found the entire family dead. On yet another visit, Procita said that DeFeo fingered Tony Mazzeo as the killer, and he later repeated that Kelske had done it. Another version was that Dawn had killed them all, and he was covering for her. During his aunt's testimony, DeFeo glared at her, as if he resented her testifying for the district attorney and revealing what he probably thought were confidential family conversations. During the testimony of other prosecution witnesses, DeFeo was stoic, seemingly disinterested, often stroking his mustache and staring at women spectators in the audience seats behind him.

"I KILLED THEM ALL, YES, SIR"

During late September and early October 1975, while the DeFeo trial was underway, both the district attorney and Weber proceeded with their preparation for the insanity defense. New York law provides that a person is legally insane and not criminally responsible when, as a result of mental disease, such person does not have substantial mental capacity to know or appreciate either the nature and consequences of his or her wrongful conduct or that such conduct was in fact wrong. Psychiatric testimony is customarily presented to a jury either to prove or disprove legal insanity.

The district attorney had DeFeo examined in the jail by Dr. Harold Zolan of Massapequa, Long Island, a highly qualified and experienced forensic psychiatrist. Zolan was consulting psychiatrist at Nassau County Medical Center, attending psychiatrist at Long Island Jewish Medical Center, and a well-known lecturer on forensic psychiatry. His first examination of DeFeo was held on September 29, 1975, and, as permitted by law, a court reporter hired by the district attorney was present. DeFeo refused to answer many of Zolan's questions. When asked what had occurred the night of the murders, he said he did not recall. Zolan stopped the examination, planning to continue it at a later date. DeFeo said later that he had refused to answer the questions because he was suspicious of the female court reporter.

Weber retained Dr. Daniel Schwartz of Brooklyn, a highly qualified and experienced forensic psychiatrist, to examine DeFeo for the insanity defense. Schwartz was director of forensic psychiatry at Kings County Hospital and associate professor of psychiatry at Downstate Medical College of the State University of New York in Brooklyn. (A few years after the DeFeo trial, Schwartz came to national attention when, as the court-appointed psychiatrist, he examined David Berkowitz, the so-called "Son of Sam" serial killer in New York City. Berkowitz avoided trial by pleading guilty to six murders.)

Schwartz conducted his first examination of DeFeo in the jail on October 4, 1975, and the second on October 13, 1975. Zolan continued his examination on October 15, 1975, again with a court reporter present, and this time DeFeo cooperated by answering Zolan's questions.

Both psychiatrists questioned DeFeo about his childhood in Brooklyn and Amityville, his schooling, employment history, and his relationship with his family. When asked about the events of November 13, 1974, he told both doctors a new version of the murders. He said that he believed his family members were plotting to kill him, and that he had to kill them all in self-defense. He also told both of the doctors another version in which he first killed both parents, then Dawn killed Allison, Marc, and John with his rifle, and he killed Dawn after struggling to get the rifle from her as she was reloading it. After their examinations, both psychiatrists made written reports, giving their opinions as to DeFeo's mental state at the time of the killings. Both would testify later during the trial, stating their respective opinions to the jury.

After the district attorney completed his case, Weber presented the evidence on DeFeo's behalf through the testimony of twenty-one witnesses (plus three on rebuttal) and seventeen trial exhibits. The witnesses included, among others, DeFeo's probation officer, the attorney who represented him on his arraignment in the district court, several Brigante-Karl Buick employees, and DeFeo household employees. To support the insanity defense, a number of DeFeo's friends recounted incidents of his past conduct that they considered irrational. Richard Wyssling's testimony about trying to find DeFeo was the same as he gave at the pretrial hearing.

On November 5, 1975, DeFeo began three days of testimony on his own behalf. He assumed the witness stand, his shirt open, chest hair showing, with what appeared to be a smirk on his face and displaying a distinct "macho" attitude. Weber questioned him first as to his schooling, employment history, and his relationship with his family. DeFeo said that as a teenager he had been thrown out of the several schools he had attended in Brooklyn, Riverhead, and Amityville for disruptive behavior and had never finished high school. He described his extensive alcohol and drug use beginning as a teenager and his frequent fighting with others.

DeFeo held a variety of jobs over the years, but he said he left most of them because he didn't get along with his superiors or was dismissed for frequent absences. As to his automobile service job at Brigante-Karl Buick, he stated that he liked it because his boss was his father and he could get away with a lot. He described always being indulged by his parents—with a car, a boat, and as much money as he wanted. He loved his parents, he said, but was never allowed by his father to move out of the family home, and he fought with him over this restriction. One incident he recounted happened in September 1973, just over a year before the murders, when he was angered by his father and threatened him with a loaded shotgun. Though he aimed and fired the gun, it failed to fire. His father, believing a divine miracle had occurred, became very religious, DeFeo said, often praying the rosary and placing ceramic religious statues in the front yard.

DeFeo's description of his interrogation by the police on November 13 and November 14, 1974, was, to an extent, the same testimony he gave on the pretrial hearing. He repeated his claim of being denied access to an attorney and said he signed the eight-page written statement only after being told they would let him go. However, there were two major differences from his hearing testimony: He did not deny telling the police he had killed his entire family, and he made no claim of police brutality. In my opinion, DeFeo, knowing that his police brutality claim was not credited by me in the pretrial hearing, probably thought that he would have a much harder time trying to get twelve jurors to believe the story. In any event, he was about to tell the jury that he, acting alone, had in fact killed his entire family.

When asked by Weber, "Ronnie, did you kill your father?" DeFeo responded, "Did I kill him? I killed them all, yes, sir, I killed them all in self-defense." At that point of the trial, we had a judicial admission of guilt right on the stand. The issue of whether or not DeFeo did the crime was now moot. Weber followed up with, "Anyone help you, Ronnie?" and DeFeo answered, "No, sir." Asked by Weber why he had killed them, he replied, "As far as I'm concerned, if I didn't kill my family, they were going to kill me … What I did was self-defense, and there was nothing wrong with it." Weber asked, "Have there been other persons who have been threats to your life?" DeFeo responded, "There have been a lot of people who have been threats to my life. I tried to find them and kill them. I might have killed a dozen people before this. I don't know."

"Are you telling us, Ronnie, that you may have killed others besides your family?" Weber asked, and DeFeo said, "It's quite possible. When I get a gun in my hand, there's no doubt in my mind who I am. I am God." (I glanced at the jury during this colloquy, and they appeared to be shocked by DeFeo's statements.) Asked by Weber how he knew of the family threats, DeFeo said that several days before the killings, he overheard his family members talking in his parents' bedroom, plotting to kill him, and that he knew then that his life was in danger.

DeFeo went on to describe another version of the killings. He said that his sister Dawn wanted to leave secretarial school and join her boyfriend in Florida, and she asked him to kill her parents because they forbade her from doing this. He was sleeping in the television room when he was awakened by Dawn, who was holding his loaded Marlin rifle (which appeared to him to be black). After Dawn handed him the gun and left the room, he went to his parents' bedroom, shot them both (though, he said, he did not hear the shots), and left the rifle on the bedroom floor.

DeFeo testified that he returned to the television room and soon heard other shots. Coming out, he saw Dawn leaving Marc and John's room with the rifle. Following her up to her bedroom, he found her reloading the rifle and got it away from her. He testified that he pushed Dawn back onto her bed and shot her in the head (though, he said, he again didn't hear that shot). Hearing footsteps, he ran downstairs, opened the front door, and saw someone running across the lawn. He described collecting the various items, putting them into the pillowcase, leaving the house, tossing the rifle into the water, driving to Brooklyn, and throwing the pillowcase into the storm drain. He denied that he changed his clothes or put any clothing into the pillowcase.

DeFeo said the lights in the house were not on during the killings or the events afterward. Was he claiming that he fatally shot his parents using the dim and flickering light cast by the single votive candle in their bedroom? Was he claiming that he fatally shot his younger siblings using any light cast into their bedrooms from night-lights left on in the bathrooms? The police did find a flashlight on the floor of the second-floor hallway. Was DeFeo claiming that he held the flashlight in one hand while aiming and firing the rifle with the other? Also, one wonders how he managed to find and pick up eight scattered, empty cartridge cases in the dark. DeFeo never answered these questions during his testimony.

DeFeo was extensively cross-examined by Sullivan. He admitted lying to the police during their initial questioning at the crime scene and later at the First Precinct and Fourth Squad headquarters. He also admitted that he never told the police that he had killed his family in self-defense or that he believed they were plotting to kill him. Sullivan widely questioned him about discrepancies between his direct testimony on trial, the things he told Zolan in jail during his psychiatric examinations, and what he said during his pretrial hearing testimony.

Before the trial, the district attorney's investigators had found out about an alleged robbery on November 1, 1974, in Brooklyn. DeFeo claimed he had been robbed at gunpoint while taking Brigante-Karl Buick cash and checks to deposit at a nearby bank. DeFeo had refused to cooperate with the New York City police officers who were investigating the alleged robbery, and Ronald DeFeo Sr. accused his son of lying about any robbery and having stolen the money himself. Sullivan questioned DeFeo about the alleged Brooklyn robbery, and he denied having any confrontation with his father about it.

DeFeo testified that his father knew the phony robbery had never taken place and that his son had stolen the money. DeFeo began to brag to the jury about how he and his father ripped off his grandfather's automobile agency by having outside body shops that did work on their customers' cars inflate their bills over the true price. Both he and his father pocketed the difference.

Sullivan accused DeFeo of killing his family to obtain large sums of money that his father had stolen from the Buick agency and

    THOMAS M. STARK

hidden. DeFeo denied this, stating, "I wouldn't kill anyone for money. If I wanted money, I'd rob a bank." Later in the cross-examination, Sullivan questioned DeFeo about his psychiatric examinations by doctors Schwartz and Zolan. DeFeo said of the two psychiatrists: "I think they're all crazy. Furthermore, I think I'm the only sane man in this courtroom." When pressed by Sullivan, he denied concocting his trial testimony or feigning insanity to avoid criminal responsibility. Becoming visibly angered, he exclaimed, "I don't give a shit what these people [the jury] find me, guilty or innocent … I either go to prison for the rest of my life or to a mental institution. What's the big deal?" Accused of fabricating his testimony, he threatened Sullivan, stating, "You think I'm playing. If I had any sense, which I don't, I'd come down there and kill you now."

At the end of his cross-examination, DeFeo, angered at Sullivan for accusing him of lying, shouted, "I tell you, you're going to see what kind of lie it is when I kill another person. I want to see what you tell the next twelve when we pick them. What are you going to tell them, it's another act? Well, you're going to be hooked up for a fucking conspiracy." The jury learned of DeFeo's foul mouth, his quickness to anger, and his resorting to bragging by these answers to Sullivan's questions, and his unsolicited outbursts showed a cavalier attitude and disdain toward his very prosecution. A reporter for the *New York Times* who attended the trial wrote in the paper that, "Only when he took the witness stand himself, did he visibly frighten jurors and spectators by exhibiting no remorse for his confessed crime." How all this affected the jury, of course, was unknown, but I believed he had hurt himself considerably.

THE *CASTLE KEEP* DEFENSE

S chwartz was the last witness called by Weber, and he was the principal witness in support of DeFeo's insanity defense. The psychiatrist began his testimony by telling the jury of his medical training, his specialization and board certification in forensic psychiatry, his hospital and teaching affiliations, and his extensive experience in examining the mental capacity of people charged with crimes. He had the appearance of the typical psychiatrist portrayed in the media: short in stature, with a mustache and a small pointed, close-clipped beard.

He testified that before he reached his conclusion as to DeFeo's legal sanity at the time of the killings, he examined him for over five hours and read many documents relating to the case. Although the documents read by Schwartz were technically what the law classifies as hearsay—that is, written information by another person who cannot be cross-examined in court as to the truth of the material contained in the document—he was permitted to rely on the contents of these documents in coming to his opinion in the DeFeo case by the ruling in a recent New York Court of Appeals decision called the *Sugden* case.

James Sugden was the defendant in a murder case tried before me in February 1972, in which he was accused of fatally stabbing and beating a thirteen-year-old with a cement block. A member of a group of young people who called themselves "God's Gifts" and hung out at a Huntington shopping center, the twenty-year-old Sugden, along with several companions, had brought the victim to an abandoned sand pit in a wooded area. Afterwards, Sugden told the others that he'd killed the boy to see if he had the nerve to do it.

Testifying at the trial that he'd taken hallucinogenic drugs and thought the victim was a giant grasshopper, his defense was legal insanity. After overruling defense counsel's objection, I permitted the forensic psychiatrist testifying for the prosecution (who coincidently happened to be Dr. Harold Zolan) to tell the jury that he had relied in part on police reports and Sugden's school and employment records in reaching his opinion.

    THOMAS M. STARK

I believed my ruling was correct under the circumstances, even though the law was not clear at the time as to whether forensic psychiatrists could use these kinds of documents (hearsay evidence) to reach an opinion as to a criminal defendant's mental condition. Sugden's murder conviction was appealed through the state court system and eventually reached the state's highest court, the Court of Appeals. In affirming Sugden's conviction, that court agreed with my trial court ruling and settled this evidence rule for future trials. When I denied that motion, I had no idea that would make statewide law.

Weber asked Schwartz to tell the jury his psychiatric opinion of DeFeo. Schwartz told the jury that, in his opinion, DeFeo was suffering from a mental disease known as paranoid psychosis at the time of the killings, and that as a result of this disease did not know that the killings were wrong. In his opinion, DeFeo was legally insane at the time and not criminally responsible for the six murders. Weber asked Schwartz to explain to the jury the basis of his opinion, and for the next fifteen minutes the jury heard an uninterrupted lecture, in which the doctor recounted what DeFeo had told him during his examination and how this supported his psychiatric opinion. Schwartz said that after DeFeo's failed attempt to shoot his father with his shotgun in September 1973, he began to have paranoid delusions regarding his relationship with others. As he came to believe that his friends were hostile toward him and ultimately that others were going to kill him, he felt he had to kill them first.

Schwartz said that this delusion became fixed on DeFeo's father as his main enemy, and then began to include his entire family. When DeFeo was in the television room at home on the night of November 12, 1974, the late movie he watched was *Castle Keep*, a 1969 World War II film starring Burt Lancaster that tells the story of a group of Allied soldiers trapped in a Rhineland castle under attack by the Germans. At the end, all the Allied soldiers were shot and killed in their attempt to defend their position. Schwartz told the jury that while he was not saying the movie caused the actual killings, he believed the movie, which contained violent fighting, led DeFeo into a paranoid belief that nothing could prevent the final violence in this case—the killing of his family to protect his own life. The movie was in effect the last straw for DeFeo.

As to DeFeo's claim that he did not hear the sound of the rifle shots, Schwartz called this "disassociation," a psychic condition wherein a person divorces himself from a certain sensory perception of reality. He said he believed DeFeo was not making this claim up, in view of his limited education and ignorance of the field of psychiatry.

Schwartz said he believed that DeFeo had, in fact, intentionally killed all six family members, and that DeFeo's description of Dawn participating in the murders was also a delusion. The psychiatrist was convinced that DeFeo was not feigning insanity.

Sullivan's cross-examination of Schwartz largely concerned questioning of the methodology he used to come to his opinions regarding DeFeo's mental capacity. Sullivan had obtained transcripts of Schwartz's insanity defense testimony in other murder trials in Nassau County and New York City. He referred to those transcripts in asking Schwartz about differences between his diagnostic methods used in those cases and the method he used in the DeFeo case. He was attempting to have Schwartz acknowledge that he used an inaccurate method in DeFeo's case, but Schwartz strongly defended his methods and diagnosis in this case.

In 1974, the law stated that when a defendant raised the insanity defense and presented evidence on trial supporting such defense, the district attorney had the burden of disproving the defense (the law has since been changed to require the defendant to prove this defense on trial). Therefore, in the DeFeo trial, the district attorney was required to disprove DeFeo's claim that he was legally insane when he committed the murders. To do this, Sullivan had to present evidence that questioned the credibility of Schwartz's opinions, as well as the credibility of DeFeo's testimony that he was not feigning insanity.

THE INSANITY DEFENSE
REJECTED

To rebut the insanity claim, Sullivan called four witnesses who had conversed with DeFeo in the jail before the trial started. He also called Zolan, whose psychiatric opinion differed from Schwartz's. For six months while awaiting trial, DeFeo was separated from the general jail population and confined to the sickbay because of rumors that he might be harmed by other inmates angered by the fact that he was accused of killing four children. Sickbay was a small section of the jail, containing only a few cells that could be watched simultaneously by one correction officer. DeFeo became friendly with three of the officers assigned to sickbay—James DeVito, Emile Ross, and Vincent D'Augusta—and talked with them openly about his case and the upcoming trial.

Correction officer DeVito testified that when DeFeo was first confined to sickbay in November 1974, he claimed that his grandfather, Rocco DeFeo, and his great uncle, Peter DeFeo, were mob-connected and out to get him—they had even arranged to have his food from the jail kitchen poisoned. According to DeVito, DeFeo spoke of another murder defendant who he said was successful in faking insanity on trial, and he told DeVito, "If he can do it, I can do it." If DeVito could come to the trial, DeFeo said, he would see a "great act when he faked insanity." DeFeo also claimed he would get out of a mental hospital in a few years and collect his family's life insurance. DeVito testified that DeFeo asked him to note in the daily log observations that he acted bizarrely so he could present these records in his trial. Correction officers Ross and D'Augusta also testified that DeFeo told them that he intended to fake insanity on trial.

John Kramer was an inmate awaiting trial who first met DeFeo when he was sent to sickbay in March 1975 and occupied the cell adjoining DeFeo. He testified that DeFeo told him of the phony robbery of the

Brigante-Karl Buick bank deposit, admitting that he had stolen the cash and that his father had been furious with him over it. DeFeo told him he would "beat the rap" (the murder case) by faking insanity and be out in a few years. As to the murders, Kramer said DeFeo first said he had not been involved but later admitted he had committed the crimes.

On one occasion, Kramer said, DeFeo told him that he had taken more than $200,000 from a hidden cash box in the house the night before the murders, intending to use the money to take off with his girlfriend, and that his father had discovered the money missing and fought with him over it. (The police found the hidden cash box in a space under the doorsill of the master bedroom closet. It was empty and wiped clean of any fingerprints.) Kramer testified that DeFeo told him that after he started the killings he went berserk and shot them all.

The testimony of the correction officers was straightforward, and there appeared to be no reason for the jury to question its truthfulness. Kramer, however, had been promised a benefit for his testimony: the district attorney would recommend to the judge a more lenient sentence in his case. The jury could consider this benefit in evaluating Kramer's testimony.

Dr. Harold Zolan was a silver-haired, dignified man who preferred to testify in the question-and-answer form. Commencing his testimony, he told the jury of his medical training, his specialization and board certification in forensic psychiatry, his hospital affiliations, and his extensive experience, similar to that of Schwartz, in examining the mental capacity of persons charged with crimes. He said he knew Schwartz well and had testified in other cases where he was involved, sometimes concurring with his opinions and other times differing.

In addition to examining DeFeo for nearly five hours, Zolan had also read many documents relating to the case, as permitted by the previously mentioned *Sugden* rule. He explained to the jury certain basic psychiatric definitions and nomenclature, that a psychosis is a form of serious mental illness in which abnormal symptoms and conduct are exhibited, such as schizophrenia, manic/depressive disease, and paranoia. He described antisocial personality as a personality disorder, not a mental disease.

Zolan told the jury that in his opinion DeFeo, at the time of the murders, was not psychotic, nor suffering from any mental disease. He found no evidence of paranoia in DeFeo's conduct at the time of the murders, but he did find much that showed him that DeFeo knew the killings were wrong, including DeFeo's careful collection and secreting of the evidence that would connect him with the crimes. DeFeo knew what he was doing in killing his family members, the psychiatrist said. DeFeo was not legally insane. His testimony demonstrated a need to impress, an unmistakable bravado and contempt for the trial itself.

Based on what DeFeo had told him during his examinations, what the records showed, and DeFeo's outbursts during his trial testimony, Zolan concluded that DeFeo had an antisocial personality. DeFeo exhibited the most common characteristics of this disorder: a low frustration level, easily aroused, frequent explosive conduct, a desire to get his own way, not accepting and fitting into the norms of society, little capacity to feel guilt, self-centered and having disregard for the feelings of others, self-gratification in his conduct, a desire to be a "big man," and a "macho" attitude. He believed DeFeo's antisocial personality, along with his rebellion against a demanding father, was one of the causes of the shootings.

Zolan did not believe the movie *Castle Keep* had anything to do with the shootings. As for DeFeo's testimony that his family and others were about to kill him and that he killed in self-defense, Zolan considered that a fabrication. Plus, in his opinion, DeFeo made up the version he told of Dawn killing the younger sister and brothers. Overall, Zolan believed DeFeo was malingering and trying to feign insanity. He, like Schwartz, said that in his opinion DeFeo had, in fact, intentionally killed all six family members. Weber's cross-examination of Zolan was wide-ranging, but it did not change his opinions.

Prior to trial DeFeo gave notice that he intended to raise the rather unique defense of having acted under the influence of extreme emotional disturbance. This isn't a defense that shows lack of criminal responsibility, such as the insanity defense. Rather, it's a mitigating defense, which allows the jury to reduce the crime of murder to manslaughter. This defense was not seriously pursued at the trial, and both forensic psychiatrists agreed that the murders were committed in a calm, deliberate manner, with no exhibition of any disturbed emotion.

The trial testimony ended with DeFeo being recalled by Weber to deny, among other things, that he acted bizarrely in jail to simulate insanity. At the end of his final cross-examination, Sullivan accused him of such conduct, and DeFeo asserted, "I had no reason to do something like that. I can't see why?" Sullivan replied, "The fact that the rest of your life depends upon this defense is no reason at all, is that correct, Mr. DeFeo?" DeFeo answered, "Mr. Sullivan, I couldn't care less what happens in this courtroom."

After nearly six weeks of testimony, the trial proceeded to the attorneys' summations to the jury. Weber spoke first, concentrating on the insanity defense and not disputing that his client had killed his entire family. He argued there was no reason to reject Schwartz's opinion. Sullivan followed, arguing that the prosecution had disproved DeFeo's insanity defense and showed that DeFeo was pretending to be insane. He emphasized that Schwartz's opinion was based on DeFeo having told him the truth; and because the prosecution had shown that DeFeo was fabricating his story, the opinion should be rejected.

My instructions to the jury were quite lengthy and comprehensive. I have always attempted to make complex legal rules and criminal law more understandable to a jury by avoiding technical legal terms and explaining matters in layman's language as much as possible. I explained the basic principles of criminal law that apply in all criminal jury trials— the presumption of the defendant's innocence; the burden of proof upon the district attorney; the standard of proof required to convict, that is, proof beyond a reasonable doubt; that the jurors are the sole judges of the facts, and that they, the jury, determine the belief to be given to each witness's testimony. I instructed them that they must determine whether the police denied DeFeo access to an attorney, which would determine whether his prearrest statements were voluntary. I told them what must be proved to convict DeFeo of intentional murder and explained the law concerning the insanity defense.

The jury deliberated for three days. At the time of the DeFeo trial, the law did not permit the members of a criminal jury to separate during deliberations, so Suffolk County had to provide meals and overnight accommodations. (The law has since been changed to permit deliberating jurors to separate during overnight and luncheon recesses.) On several occasions, the jury returned to the courtroom to have testimony read back by the court reporter or for a repeating or clarification of a particular point of law. On November 21, 1975, the jury announced its verdicts. The courtroom was crowded with police officers, relatives of jury members (who were probably curious what their missing family member had been doing those three days), court buffs, the three remaining alternate jurors (who had not been substituted into the regular jury), and members of the media.

Jury foreman Mary Astromovich stood and, answering the clerk's questions, reported the six verdicts (one for each victim): guilty of murder as charged. The guilty verdicts, in effect, rejected the insanity defense. If the jury had found that the defense had not been disproved, the required verdict would have been not guilty by reason of mental disease or defect. DeFeo showed no visible reaction to the verdicts. Weber requested that the individual jurors be polled, and the clerk asked each if this was his or her verdict (again six times). Moments later, as part of a routine series of post-verdict questions, the clerk asked DeFeo, "Are your parents living?" The *Newsday* reporter in the courtroom wrote that DeFeo "gave a short, shrill laugh and then answered calmly, 'No, sir.'"

None of DeFeo's relatives attended the rendering of the verdicts or the subsequent sentencing. Nor had any relatives attended any of the trial sessions as spectators. DeFeo's grandfather, Michael Brigante Sr., and uncle, Michael Brigante Jr., had testified early in the trial, but neither remained as a spectator thereafter.

I thanked the jury for their exceptional service—at that time the DeFeo case was the longest murder trial in the county's history—and discharged them. Some left the courthouse through a rear employee entrance to avoid the press, while others left through the lobby, where several willingly spoke to the press. Several jurors revealed details of the deliberations (no law forbids this). After the initial discussion, the first vote was ten to two for conviction. The two jurors who disagreed were not sure whether DeFeo was legally insane when he committed the crimes, and the subsequent deliberations focused on the insanity issue.

On the second day, the next vote was eleven to one for conviction. The following morning the remaining juror, who was still not sure, asked for Detective Rafferty's testimony to be read back, the portion recounting how DeFeo had described committing the murders. Upon returning to the jury room, the juror agreed to a unanimous vote to convict. There was never any disagreement among the jurors as to DeFeo being the person who shot and intentionally killed all six family members.

After the verdict, I ordered the required presentence investigation and report and fixed the sentencing date. During the following two weeks, a county probation department officer interviewed homicide squad detectives, Sullivan, DeFeo, his former probation officer, his grandfather Brigante, and others, and these interviews were summarized and reported to me. The presentence report also contained an overall evaluation of DeFeo, stating that he exhibited an aura of macho and that he had a history of misrepresenting, fabricating, fantasizing and of being overindulged and overprotected by his family. The probation department recommended that I extend no leniency in view of the seriousness and nature of his crimes and that I impose the maximum prison sentence.

I had observed and listened to DeFeo as he testified and was satisfied that he was an antisocial individual who was self-centered and had little regard for others. In my opinion, DeFeo's differing versions of the killings were obvious attempts to avoid criminal responsibility for the shocking murders of his six family members. I believed that he told the truth in his incriminating admissions to the homicide squad detectives on the afternoon of November 14, 1974, well before his thoughts and plans of a trial strategy began to form.

The sentencing proceeding on December 4, 1975, followed the procedure required by state law: the district attorney's and defense counsel's statements, DeFeo being offered an opportunity to address me (he chose not to at the outset, but later, on noting his intention to appeal his sentence, announced, "I believe I'll be back here within a year"), and my summary of the factors I considered in determining his sentence. Urging that I show no mercy, Sullivan described the crime as "an event so appalling and cataclysmic that it is without equal." Weber, for his part, argued that "this act itself was an act of insanity."

I described the killings as being carried out in a calm, callous, and unfeeling manner, as DeFeo went quickly from room to room, firing a high-powered rifle at close range into areas of each victim's body where he knew wounds would be fatal. As I told the courtroom, "The crimes committed in this case are the most heinous and abhorrent known to the community, the deliberate taking of human lives." In addition to his own statement, there was tremendous evidence indicating consciousness of guilt—throwing away the gun, carefully collecting and secreting the evidence that would connect him with the crimes. This indicated his knowledge that was he did was wrong, both in the legal and moral sense. And, ultimately, he attempted to avoid criminal responsibility by feigning insanity.

I stated my intention to impose life sentences with the longest minimum period possible and gave my reasons: to demonstrate to the community that the punishments specified in New York State's criminal law cannot be ignored without consequences, that the state is determined to uphold norms of conduct by forceful action taken against wrongdoers, and that because of DeFeo's history and character, he is a danger to the community and must be confined for a long period of time.

I then imposed six sentences of life imprisonment, each with a minimum of twenty-five years. I also directed that the six sentences run consecutively with respect to each other. I knew that this direction of consecutive sentences was not binding on the state correctional authorities, but I wanted to indicate my belief that DeFeo should not be paroled early. On the following day, DeFeo was driven by the county sheriff to the New York state prison at Ossining and became state inmate number 75A4053.

In 1975, the prison at Ossining (known as "Sing Sing") was the receiving prison for sentenced felons from New York City and the metropolitan area, including Long Island and the lower Hudson River Valley. Arriving inmates were classified according to the nature of their offense and length of sentence, and then transferred to the appropriate prison in the state system. DeFeo remained confined in New York's maximum-security prisons for the rest of his life.

FRUITLESS APPEALS

Between 1975 and 1984, DeFeo pursued appeals in the New York state and federal courts. None of the appeals were successful. His first appeal was to the Appellate Division of the Supreme Court in Brooklyn. This is an intermediate appellate court to which all felony convictions on Long Island may be appealed. It has broad powers and may affirm or reverse convictions, order new trials, dismiss indictments, or reduce sentences. The court is not required to give reasons for decisions affirming convictions but may do so in a written opinion.

Attorney William E. Weber, having represented DeFeo on trial, continued to represent him on this appeal. The administrators of the DeFeo estates agreed to pay Weber $20,000 for his services and expenses. Michael Brigante Sr., who had a legal interest in the victims' estates, apparently approved this payment. Did Brigante believe DeFeo, who had now been convicted and sentenced for the killing of his daughter, his son-in-law, and four of his grandchildren, was innocent, or did he believe DeFeo somehow had been wrongfully convicted? It is simply possible that he still had affection for his grandson, regardless of his beliefs, and wanted him to have a competent appeal. During the trial, when I'd allowed Brigante to approach DeFeo after testifying, he hugged and kissed his grandson, saying something to him in English and Italian, onlookers reported. Michael Brigante Sr. is now deceased.

Mark D. Cohen, chief appellate attorney of the district attorney's office, handled the appeals on behalf of the prosecution. Over the following two years the entire trial record, plus DeFeo's and the district attorney's briefs containing their arguments, were printed, and all these documents were filed in the appellate division. Weber's seventy-seven-page brief was extensive, setting forth numerous reasons why DeFeo's conviction should be reversed. He also sought to reduce the sentence as being excessive.

Weber's principal arguments were (1) that my decision after the pretrial hearing finding DeFeo's oral and written statements to the police were voluntarily made was legally incorrect and should be reversed, (2) that my jury instructions concerning the insanity defense were inadequate and erroneous, and (3) that the prosecution failed to disprove the defense. He also reargued my refusal to delay the trial and claimed I made other errors, which, taken together, denied DeFeo a fair trial. Cohen's seventy-two-page brief responded to DeFeo's claims. He argued that my pretrial hearing decision and jury instructions were correct, that the prosecution had disproved the insanity defense, and that the sentence was appropriate and should not be reduced.

The appeal was orally argued before the Appellate Division on March 9, 1978. Before the arguments, the four justices who heard the appeal—Vito Titone, Sam Rabin, Charles Margett, and Frank Gulotta—had read the briefs and considered the reports of court attorneys who had researched the legal issues and read the trial record. They were thus well familiar with the issues and able to question the attorneys during oral arguments. They later voted unanimously to affirm DeFeo's convictions, choosing not to write an opinion, and filed their written decision on March 27, 1978. DeFeo sought permission to appeal the Appellate Division decision to the New York Court of Appeals in Albany, the state's highest court. This court permits such appeals only if there is a question of state law to be reviewed. On May 23, 1978, Chief Judge Charles Breitel of that court denied DeFeo's application.

DeFeo's next appeal was to the federal courts. Under the United States Code, a state prisoner may petition a federal district court for a writ of habeas corpus to challenge his conviction on constitutional grounds. In 1982, DeFeo was an inmate at Clinton Correctional Facility at Dannemora, New York. The prison provided him with a printed habeas corpus petition, which contained detailed instructions for how to complete and file it. The form also listed the ten most-frequently raised grounds for habeas corpus relief, and space was provided for the inmate to state each ground on which he claimed he was being unlawfully held and set forth the facts supporting such ground. I was surprised to learn that New York State provided such documents. It seemed to be encouraging inmates to deluge the federal courts with self-composed habeas corpus petitions, resulting in time-consuming and expensive processing and investigation by court officials to determine whether the petitions have sufficient merit to be assigned to a district court judge.

DeFeo's petition listed two grounds: that his right to counsel under the sixth amendment to the constitution was violated by the police, and that his privilege against self-incrimination under the Fifth Amendment was also violated by the police. To support these grounds, he largely stated the same facts he had claimed in the pretrial hearing before me in 1975. DeFeo's petition, together with a memorandum of law written by him, was filed in the clerk's office of the United States District Court in Brooklyn. (That court's district included Suffolk County, his place of conviction.)

Because of DeFeo's indigence, the law firm of Sullivan and Cromwell of New York City was assigned to represent him. This was a large Wall Street firm, and one of the firm's associate attorneys, Jeh Charles Johnson, was assigned by the managing partner to DeFeo's case (decades later Johnson would go on to serve as U.S. Secretary of Homeland Security). Johnson obtained and read the trial record and prepared a memorandum of law in support of those of DeFeo's complaints that he believed should be submitted to the court. The Suffolk County District Attorney responded to Johnson's legal arguments, and all the documents, including the trial record, were then considered by District Judge Leonard D. Wexler.

On May 16, 1984, the judge filed an eight-page decision. He summarized the facts of DeFeo's interrogation by the police on the night of November 13, 1974, his original written statement, DeFeo becoming a suspect the following morning, being given his Miranda warnings, his waiver of his rights, and his ultimate admission of murdering his family. Judge Wexler referred to my findings after the pretrial hearing that DeFeo was not in police custody until the morning of November 14, when he did become a suspect and was given his Miranda warnings. He determined that the principal issue before him was whether DeFeo voluntarily and intelligently waived his privilege against self-incrimination. DeFeo's attorney argued that his client was effectively "in custody" on the night of November 13, being "psychologically" restrained by the police at that time. Judge Wexler rejected this contention and found that DeFeo knowingly and intelligently waived his constitutional rights on the morning of November 14, before further interrogation. He saw no reason to conduct a new hearing to develop any other facts concerning the police interrogation, stating that DeFeo had received a full and complete hearing before me. DeFeo's petition for a writ of habeas corpus was denied.

DeFeo's attorney appealed Judge Wexler's denial to the United States Court of Appeals for the Second Circuit in New York City. Along with assistant district attorney Cohen, he agreed on a joint appendix containing the applicable parts of the trial record to submit to the court, and both parties filed briefs on the issues. The attorneys orally argued before the court, and on October 19, 1984, the three appellate circuit judges rendered their decision. In a comprehensive opinion, they found that the district attorney demonstrated that DeFeo knowingly and intelligently waived his constitutional rights, and they agreed with my finding that DeFeo was not in police custody until he became a suspect on the morning of November 14. They agreed with Judge Wexler that a new hearing was not required. Accordingly, they unanimously affirmed Wexler's decision denying a writ of habeas corpus. The circuit court decision effectively ended DeFeo's direct appeals from his convictions. He made no effort to take the case to the United States Supreme Court. There being no novel issue of constitutional law presented, it was unlikely that that court would grant certiorari permitting an appeal.

BACK TO RIVERHEAD

At this point, to further challenge his convictions DeFeo had to utilize Article 440 of the New York Criminal Procedure Law, which permits a convicted defendant, under certain limited circumstances, to bring a proceeding to vacate a judgment of conviction. DeFeo, by the late 1980s, had become very astute concerning the law and familiar with New York criminal procedure, and he chose to commence a proceeding in the Supreme Court of Suffolk County seeking to vacate his convictions under the provisions of Article 440. At the time, he was an inmate in Sullivan Correctional Facility at Fallsburg, New York, and he used the prison law library to prepare his application, assisted by William Shaffer, a prison law assistant.

On March 20, 1990, he sent the Supreme Court clerk at Riverhead a lengthy document containing ten sworn affidavits, including his own and those of nine other individuals, and sent duplicate copies to the district attorney. The proceeding was assigned to me because I had been the trial judge in 1975. DeFeo now chose to blame his trial attorney, William Weber, for his convictions. His overall claim was that Weber's conduct, before and during his trial, was improper and deprived him of effective assistance of counsel. He listed five incidents of Weber's alleged misconduct, and also claimed that he had newly discovered evidence that would have made a difference in the jury's verdicts.

His principal claim was that Weber prevented him during trial from presenting the truth of what occurred the night of the murders. According to his new story, on November 13, 1974, he was living with a wife and infant daughter in Long Branch, New Jersey, when his mother telephoned him to say that Dawn was fighting with his father and asked him to come to Amityville. He claimed that he and his brother-in-law, Richard Romondoe, drove to the house in Amityville and, finding the fight was over, went to the basement to play pool and watch television. After hearing gunshots, they went upstairs and found his parents, Allison, Marc, and John dead of gunshot wounds. He encountered Dawn holding his Marlin rifle and, during a struggle to take it from her, it discharged, killing Dawn. Then he and Romondoe left the house, threw the rifle into the Amityville Creek, and returned to New Jersey.

In his affidavit, he also claimed that he did not want to use the insanity defense on trial, but Weber forced him to do so. Weber also instructed many of his witnesses to falsely testify as to him acting irrationally, DeFeo contended, and told Romondoe that he could not attend the trial and testify to the true facts. DeFeo said that Weber's conduct at the trial was motivated by a plan to profit from book and movie rights. Among the sworn affidavits DeFeo filed were those of his alleged wife and alleged brother-in-law, both supporting what he claimed happened in 1974.

The district attorney looked into DeFeo's claims of a marriage and the existence of a brother-in-law. The investigators interviewed Geraldine Gates of Deposit, New York, the woman who DeFeo claimed was his wife at the time of the murders. She told them she had received her affidavit and that of a "Richard Romondoe" from DeFeo. Both were already completed, hers using the name "Geraldine DeFeo" and the Romondoe affidavit already signed with that name. After signing her affidavit, she took both affidavits to a friend who notarized the documents and then returned them to DeFeo. She said the facts in her affidavit were entirely false.

In March 1990 Gates was brought to the district attorney's office in Hauppauge, where she signed an affidavit containing what she said were the true facts—and then another affidavit two months later, modifying it. In the first affidavit, she said she had never been married to DeFeo and that she had first met him in the 1980s, when she was married to Gerald Gates, her present husband. She had no brother named Richard Romondoe. In the second one, Gates conceded that she had married DeFeo a year earlier.

The district attorney's opposition documents to DeFeo's Article 440 application included the Geraldine Gates affidavit recanting her original affidavit. The prosecutor submitted papers describing the lengthy investigation of the alleged brother-in-law, "Richard Romondoe." A nationwide search revealed no driver license for anyone with that name, nor any credit report. No phone was listed for a Richard Romondoe in and around New Jersey. The landlady at the building Gates gave as their address never rented to her or Romondoe. DeFeo had fabricated his very existence, the district attorney contended, as well as the version of events described in Romondoe's "signed" affidavit. When DeFeo received a copy of the affidavit Geraldine Gates signed for the district attorney, he convinced her to sign *another* affidavit recanting the one she gave the district attorney.

DeFeo was entitled by law to have an evidentiary hearing in court, in which he had the burden of proving the truth of his claims. He was also entitled, due to his indigence, to have an attorney appointed, at public expense, to conduct the hearing and present his evidence. Over the following months, I appointed, in succession, four different qualified attorneys to represent DeFeo. I had to relieve the first two because DeFeo disagreed with them and refused to consider their advice. The third withdrew due to the press of other business. The fourth attorney, Gerald Lotto, was able to get along with DeFeo. Angela Brigante, DeFeo's maternal grandmother, advanced $10,000 to pay any investigative and scientific testing expenses for her grandson, and this was approved by the administrator of the assigned counsel plan, as long as none of these funds would be paid to Lotto for his services.

DeFeo was brought from prison to the Suffolk County jail for the six-day hearing, which was held before me in June 1992. Thirteen witnesses, including DeFeo, testified, and twelve documents, including the trial transcript, were admitted into evidence. After the conclusion of the hearing, while I was reviewing and considering the evidence, DeFeo, now back in prison, advised me that he was dissatisfied with Lotto's conduct at the hearing and wanted nothing more to do with him. Under these circumstances, I relieved Lotto and declined to appoint another attorney.

On January 6, 1993, I rendered my lengthy decision, denying DeFeo's Article 440 application to vacate his convictions. I found that DeFeo's hearing testimony that he was married, with child, and living in New Jersey in November 1974, was false and fabricated. It was totally

     THOMAS M. STARK

incredible. He produced no corroborating evidence, such as a marriage certificate or a child's birth certificate showing him to be the father. He also failed to present live testimony by his alleged wife or his alleged brother-in-law. What's more, immediately after the murders he signed a statement describing how he lived at home with his parents and siblings and regularly commuted to and from work with his father. At his original trial, his girlfriend, Mindy Weiss, testified that they had been dating since June 1974 and saw each other frequently that summer and fall.

I also judged DeFeo's testimony of not having killed his parents and siblings to be false. This claim was contradicted by the trial evidence, DeFeo's previous incriminatory admissions, and the affirmed jury verdict. In addition, I determined that DeFeo had fully cooperated with Weber in presenting the insanity defense and that there was no proof of attorney misconduct by Weber. My decision could only be appealed by permission of the Appellate Division, and DeFeo sought such permission. That court, after reviewing my decision and DeFeo's application, declined to permit an appeal.

After his unsuccessful Article 440 proceeding, DeFeo reverted to one of his earlier versions of the killings: that he killed his parents, Dawn then killed the three younger siblings and he killed Dawn after the struggle for the rifle. He unsuccessfully sought a court order seeking scientific analysis of Dawn's nightgown to demonstrate she had fired the rifle shots killing Allison, Marc, and John. He also unsuccessfully attempted to reopen his allegations of police brutality, claiming the police had switched his blood-stained clothing, which would have corroborated the beating.

By November 14, 1999, DeFeo had served his minimum twenty-five-year sentence and became eligible to be considered for release on parole. The New York Board of Parole consists of nineteen commissioners, who sit in three-member panels for each parole application. Panel membership is rotated, and their meetings at the various state prisons are also rotated. The panel interviews the inmate and reviews the case record, the inmate's disciplinary record, his institutional adjustment, and any release plans.

Starting in 1999, DeFeo was interviewed by panels at Green Haven Correctional Facility in Stormville, New York. There were eight interviews at two-year intervals, and each panel, consisting of different commissioners, unanimously denied parole. During each interview, DeFeo denied murdering all six family members, the crimes for which he was convicted and sentenced. (Since this book was written, DeFeo was denied parole three more times, most recently in 2019.)

In their written decisions denying parole, the panels stated their reasons, which included: DeFeo's refusal to accept full responsibility for the murders by giving various versions of his involvement and minimizing his own conduct; his lack of insight into the brutality of his conduct; his failure to show remorse for killing innocent and defenseless victims; the heinous nature of his killings, which demonstrated DeFeo's depraved indifference to human life; that his release would depreciate the serious nature of the killings and undermine respect for law; that if he were to be released it was reasonably probable that he would violate the law; and that he remained dangerous to public safety.

On March 12, 2021, while incarcerated at the Sullivan Correctional Facility, Ronald DeFeo Jr. died at nearby Albany Medical Center. He was sixty-nine years old.

THE HISTORY OF THE HOAX

During 1975 the DeFeo house in Amityville remained vacant. The furnishings were removed by the administrators of the DeFeo estates, and the house was listed for sale through a real estate agent for $80,000 (a bargain in view of its size and waterfront location). In the fall, the house was shown to George and Kathleen Lutz, who had recently married. It was Kathleen's second marriage, and she had three young children. The house had space for a growing family, and the finished basement could be used by George as an office for his land surveying business.

After they expressed interest in the house, the agent told them it was the site of the DeFeo family murders, but this did not deter them. The price was more than they had planned to spend, but if they could obtain a large mortgage, they would go ahead. Columbia Savings and Loan Association approved the loan, and the Lutzes purchased the house and moved in on December 18, 1975. Less than one month later, on January 14, 1976, the Lutzes moved out of the house. The combined mortgage payments, real estate taxes, and insurance costs were high, and they found they had misgivings about living in the house where the murders had taken place. Lutz, wanting to find out more about the history of the DeFeo house and the murders, met with DeFeo's attorney, William Weber, later in January.

In a local radio station interview several years later, Weber recounted what had occurred at that first meeting. He said George Lutz questioned him about the house and the murders and told him about his and his wife's unusual foreboding and nervousness while living in the very rooms where the murders had taken place, as well as their belief that the house was in some manner haunted. Saying he was interested in Lutzes' haunted-house story, Weber suggested that Lutz could describe his experience of briefly living in the house in a book Weber and his associates were planning to write about the DeFeo murders and trial. Lutz signed an agreement to participate in the Weber book project. During the following weeks, Weber and Lutz met frequently and had lengthy discussions concerning the house, the murders and the trial. Weber said he and Lutz began to embellish and exaggerate the Lutzes' experiences into an extensive haunted-house version, with the Lutz family fleeing the house because of psychic events and other phenomena. In a later on-air interview with television reporter Marvin Scott, Weber said several bottles of wine helped the story along.

The Weber group hired Paul Hoffman to publicize the now-expanded Lutz story and eventually write the DeFeo book. On February 14, the Long Island newspaper *Newsday* printed the haunted-house story

("DeFeo House Abandoned; Buyer Calls It Haunted"). The same day a *Daily News* story asked, "Is Murder House Haunted?" Curious readers began congregating around the Ocean Avenue house, hoping to see the reported ghosts. Two days later, the Lutzes conducted a press conference at Weber's office, and the lawyer remarked that these new developments could possibly merit a new trial. A reporter from New York's Channel 5 television visited the property and spoke with the Lutzes, and in March the station broadcast an overnight séance held in the house, which had been sanctioned by the Lutzes (who still owned the property).

Soon after publishing its original article, *Newsday* contacted Stephen Kaplan of Setauket, Long Island, head of the Parapsychology Institute of America, and sought his opinion about the story. He said he couldn't weigh in without a professional investigation of the house. Seeing Kaplan's name in *Newsday*, George Lutz reached out to the parapsychologist and asked him to investigate. Kaplan agreed to meet Lutz several days later, but when Lutz cancelled Kaplan began to suspect that the whole story was a hoax, as his investigation probably would have revealed. His suspicion was confirmed when Channel 5 broadcast the séance. In his 1995 book about the alleged haunting, Kaplan called the made-for-TV event a "three-ring circus" that incorporated "most of the classical stereotypes of fraudulent spiritualism."

In the subsequent months, Hoffman wrote stories about the "haunting" that were published in *The New York Sunday News* and *Good Housekeeping* magazine. The latter story resulted in people from all over driving to Amityville to visit the property, and this began to cause problems for James and Barbara Cromarty, who had purchased the house from Colonial Savings and Loan Association (the Lutzes had deeded the property to the Association when they defaulted on the mortgage payments). The Cromartys had to seek the aid of the Amityville police to keep curious trespassers off the property.

The book publisher Prentice-Hall hired author Jay Anson to interview the Lutzes and write a book about the "haunting." Rather than continue with Hoffman and the Weber group, the Lutzes agreed to work with Anson on his book. By this time the couple had moved to San Diego, California. The lengthy description of their experiences in the house that they tape-recorded for Anson contained more psychic events than previously versions had, and now specific dates were given for each event. Anson's book was published by Prentice-Hall in August 1977. Entitled *The Amityville Horror* and subtitled *A True Story*, it was 201 pages long and copyrighted by Anson and George and Kathleen Lutz.

The book opens with a short preface by a Catholic priest concerning the phenomenon of demonic possession, which the Lutzes' experiences purported to be. It continues in the form of a diary for the twenty-eight days the Lutz family occupied the house. Those days are filled with ghostly noises, unnatural chills, body levitation, black substances oozing from walls and keyholes, the sound of marching bands, the young daughter's encounter with a red-eyed pig she named "Jodie," massive swarming of flies in midwinter, furniture moving by itself, the bodily transformation of Kathleen into an old hag, and the appearance of a large, hooded figure. A Catholic priest, while blessing the house, hears a spectral voice telling him to get out and is subsequently inflicted with stigmata. An Amityville police officer investigating the house senses "strong vibrations" and has "a creepy feeling." The book ends with Anson's description of his own investigation of the Lutzes' claims, comparing them with what parapsychologists have written about similar psychic events.

The Amityville Horror soon became a national best-seller. It went to twelve printings, and sales eventually reached six million copies. Prentice Hall sent George and Kathleen Lutz on a tour of major American cities to appear at bookstores and be interviewed by local media. The couple admitted several minor inaccuracies in the book but steadfastly insisted that it was a true story. The paperback and movie rights were sold for a substantial sum. *The New York Times* syndicate division bought serialization rights for over four hundred papers, and a magazine in England purchased syndication rights for Europe and the United Kingdom. The weekly scandal sheet *National Enquirer* published a lurid account of the Lutzes' experiences entitled "The Untold Story," based on an exclusive interview with Kathleen Lutz.

Two movie versions of *The Amityville Horror* were produced. The first, in 1979, was faithful to the Lutz story but did not claim it to be true. This movie was a success by Hollywood standards—even earning an Oscar nomination for best score. The 2005 remake embellished the story with extraneous events and was not as successful. (The Amityville house also makes an appearance in 2016's *The Conjuring 2*. The sequel to 2013's *The Conjuring*, it follows the story of Ed and Lorraine Warren, the real-life paranormal investigators whose 1976 séance at the Ocean Avenue house was broadcast on Channel 5.)

The Lutzes sought to capitalize on *The Amityville Horror*'s spectacular success by claiming that the evil forces experienced in the DeFeo house had followed them to California. In three more books, the Lutzes told of these continuing psychic experiences thousands of miles from Amityville. None of these later books were as successful as the original.

The remarkable success of *The Amityville Horror* was largely attributed to the publisher's and the Lutzes' assertion that it was a true story, a tale of the supernatural events that occurred in the house where the DeFeo family murders had been committed and the supposition that the house was haunted as a result of the six horrific killings.

In the fall of 1977, *Newsday* investigated the Lutzes' claims and published a lengthy article entitled "Fact or Fiction." The reporters found that no Amityville police officer had ever visited the house, as claimed by Lutz. Nor had the Catholic priest mentioned in the book, although he knew Kathleen Lutz, ever visited or blessed the house, and he never suffered with stigmata, as claimed in the book. James Cromarty told *Newsday* that his family never had any unusual experiences while living in the house since early 1977. The Cromarty family, however, was harassed by a constant stream of tourists attempting to see the house after *The Amityville Horror* was published.

Reporters for radio station WBAB in Babylon, a town adjoining Amityville, also investigated the Lutzes' story and became convinced it was a hoax, although they had no credible evidence to announce this to their listeners. The assertion by the parapsychologist Stephen Kaplan that the entire story was a gigantic hoax fell on deaf ears, even though he advanced his claim as much as possible through the media and lectures to interested groups and organizations. Kaplan's message: The story had been sold to a public that wanted to believe in haunted houses and the presence of malevolent spirits.

THE HOAX UNRAVELS

Prior to the publication of *The Amityville Horror*, another investigation of the psychic phenomenon allegedly present in the DeFeo house was undertaken by Hans Holzer, a New York City parapsychologist. Weber had contacted Holzer in the fall of 1976 and arranged for him to visit the then-empty house on January 13, 1977 (the house had not yet been purchased by the Cromartys). Holzer was accompanied by a medium, Ethel Myers, and a television researcher. Holzer later recounted that upon entry the medium went into a trance and described to him what she was experiencing from her surroundings. His questions to her and her answers while in the trance were captured on a portable tape recorder. In the recording, she described the house as being possessed by the spirit of a long-dead Indian chief, whose grave in the vicinity had been disturbed by a child, and that this spirit had caused recent violence in the house. The medium's descriptions led Holzer to consider the possibility that DeFeo had been possessed by the vengeful spirit.

Holzer continued his investigation over the following two years by reading the murder trial record and DeFeo's appellate brief and interviewing Weber, Dr. Daniel Schwartz (the psychiatrist who testified for the defense at the trial), and DeFeo in his upstate prison. In July 1979, after being unable to revisit the now-occupied house, Holzer and the medium conducted a séance in Weber's office. During the trance, Holzer reported, the medium told him that the child who disturbed the Indian's grave was later killed by his spirit, and that the same spirit had caused DeFeo to kill his family.

After interviewing a college professor on the subject of evil possession, Holzer concluded that DeFeo, sometime after moving into the Amityville house, had become possessed by an evil force and was not acting of his own will and intention when he murdered his family. In 1979 Holzer published a book describing his investigation entitled *Murder in Amityville* (which was the basis for the 1982 film *Amityville II: The Possession*).

Around the same time Holzer was conducting his second séance, the "Amityville Horror" was finally exposed to the public as a hoax. On July 27, 1979, the day the original movie opened, the *New York Post* published an article entitled "Lawyer Claims Amityville Book was Hokum, not Horror." In it, Weber admitted that he participated with the Lutzes to create and embellish their reported psychic experiences while living in the DeFeo house. In August radio station WBAB invited Weber to be interviewed on its popular Joel Martin show, and he accepted. (The transcript of the entire two-hour interview is published in Kaplan's 1995 book, *The Amityville Horror Conspiracy*.) In the interview, Weber described his meetings with George Lutz and their conversations concerning the house. He told Martin how he helped Lutz embellish the "haunted house" story, intending to incorporate the fiction into his planned DeFeo book. He claimed that the subsequent Prentice-Hall book was made up by George and Kathleen Lutz (based to a large extent on the story he and Lutz initially created), who convinced Jay Anson that the psychic events actually happened.

Subsequently, Weber's admissions received nationwide publicity in a September 1979 *People* magazine cover story about the movie. Featuring a photo of the actress who played Kathleen Lutz in the film, the cover proclaimed, "The movie is mostly baloney, but Margot Kidder is worth shouting about." In 1988, Weber appeared on the television program, "A Current Affair," and described his role in helping the Lutzes transform real events that occurred in the DeFeo house into fictional psychic phenomena. Testifying before me in DeFeo's 1992 Supreme Court Article 440 hearing, Weber described in detail his participation

     THOMAS M. STARK

in creating the hoax. In spite of Weber's many public statements, George and Kathleen Lutz continued to insist the story was true.

During these years, the Amityville "haunted house" story generated several lawsuits. In May 1977 George and Kathleen Lutz sued Weber, Hoffman, *Good Housekeeping*, *The New York Sunday News* and the Hearst Corporation in Federal District Court in Brooklyn. They alleged that the publication of the 1976 and 1977 articles invaded their privacy, misappropriated their names for trade purposes, and caused them mental distress. Weber brought a countersuit alleging that the Lutzes had perpetuated a fraud and breached the contract to participate in the writing of his group's book when they subsequently contracted with Anson and Prentice-Hall.

The Lutzes' case against *Good Housekeeping*, *The New York Sunday News*, and the Hearst Corporation was dismissed by the judge, who found that there was no invasion of privacy in that the Lutzes themselves had initially publicized the story in television interviews and press conferences. In September 1979, after a trial of the remaining case against Weber and Hoffman, the judge dismissed that part, stating that the work was to a large extent fictional, relying a large part upon Weber's suggestions. Weber's countersuit was continued, even though the judge pointed out potential ethical questions regarding Weber's conduct when he became involved as a literary agent while still representing DeFeo and said that he had considered referring the matter to the attorney disciplinary authorities. Under the circumstances, Weber thought it best to settle his case by accepting $2,500.

James and Barbara Cromarty sued the Lutzes, Anson, and Prentice Hall for damages caused by the thousands of gawkers who flocked to their property after the publication of *The Amityville Horror*. Many came with cameras and tape recorders and asked to be admitted to the house to photograph and record the "ghosts." Others came to the door at all hours and sought to perform exorcisms to rid the house of the spirits. Some roamed all over the property, trampling the lawn and flower beds. The Cromartys had to be constantly aided by the Amityville police to remove the trespassers. They eventually settled the lawsuit for an undisclosed amount.

In 1988 DeFeo brought a lawsuit in the Federal District Court in Brooklyn against Weber, the Lutzes, Holzer, Anson's estate, and several publishers. He claimed that Weber conspired against him by exploiting his story and by presenting a false insanity defense on trial. He also claimed that the notoriety of *The Amityville Horror* denied him his rights to due process of law and that Holzer's Indian chief possession story was a fraud upon the public. District Judge Wexler dismissed DeFeo's case as not presenting any claim that could be adjudicated in the federal courts.

George and Kathleen Lutz later divorced, and George moved to Las Vegas, Nevada, where he died in May 2006. Kathleen Lutz died in 2004. William Weber continued to practice law on Long Island.

DEFEO'S WIDENING FAME

In many respects, Ronald DeFeo Jr. was not an ordinary state prisoner. For one, he had unusual connections to the world outside prison. Between 1979 and 2005, DeFeo participated in at least six interviews concerning his convictions, three of them televised. The first interview was in 1979, when Hans Holzer visited DeFeo at Clinton Correctional Facility. During that conversation, DeFeo admitted that he had killed all six members of his family, saying that he did it alone and had no help from anyone. He made no claim of self-defense and described the shootings as going quickly, producing a very loud noise. First saying that he didn't know why he did it, he eventually agreed with Holzer's suggestion that a "strange power" within him made him commit the murders. The transcript of this interview is printed in Holzer's book, *Murder in Amityville.*

In a 1986 interview with *Newsday's* Bob Keeler, DeFeo told the reporter he had been married and had a child at the time of the murders.

Sitting in a prison visiting room with Geraldine Gates at his side, DeFeo claimed that while he was downstairs with his brother-in-law Dawn shot their father, leading his distraught mother to kill Dawn and the other children before shooting herself. Hearing the shots, he came upstairs, found his mother still alive, and shot her dead.

DeFeo's first interview for television took place in Riverhead in June 1992, after the conclusion of the Supreme Court Article 440 hearing. He was interviewed in the courtroom (the sheriff forbade an interview in the jail) by Doug Geed, a news commentator on News12 Long Island. The interview was telecast during the evening news and repeated several times the following day. DeFeo basically repeated the testimony he had just given at his hearing (married with child, living in New Jersey, coming to Amityville with his brother-in-law, hearing the shooting taking place upstairs, struggling with Dawn for the rifle, and killing her when it discharged). He never told the police about his brother-in-law being present, he said, because he did not want to get him involved and possibly charged as an accomplice in Dawn's killing.

DeFeo's second on-air interview was for a television documentary program about the murders called *Deadly Minds*, which was produced in 1994. (It can now be viewed as an episode of the series, *Serial Killers*, available on Amazon Prime.) DeFeo's interview took place at Green Haven Correctional Facility in Stormville, New York. I was interviewed for the program, along with Suffolk County police detectives Dennis Rafferty and Robert Schomacker, Lieutenant Robert Dunn, police officer Kenneth Greguski (who went on to become the Amityville Chief of Police), attorney Gerald Lotto, Hans Holzer, and assistant district attorney Michael Ahearn (prosecutor Gerard Sullivan was by then deceased).

DeFeo told producer Christopher Berry-Dee that he constantly argued with his father but got along well with the rest of his family. This time around, he said he killed Dawn during an out-of-control rage after discovering that she had shot the other members of the family. The program was widely telecast on cable television channels throughout the country.

In 2002 DeFeo was interviewed by phone for the television program *Prime Time Live*. Denying the "strange power within" version of the murders he told Holzer, this time he claimed that both of his parents had abused him and that he was drunk and high on heroin when he committed the killings. (DeFeo had used the drug in the past. But as a condition of the sentence of probation he was serving for the outboard motor theft, he was required to provide weekly urine samples, which were tested for evidence of heroin and other illegal drugs, and none had been detected.)

DeFeo's next television interview was by Teale-Edwards Productions of New York City, producer of the one-hour program *First Person Killers: Ronald DeFeo*, telecast nationwide on the Arts & Entertainment Network (A&E) on April 24, 2006. I was interviewed for this program, along with Suffolk County police detectives Gaspar Randazzo and Gerard Gozaloff, firearms expert Alfred Della Penna, Dr. Howard Adelman (the forensic pathologist who conducted the autopsies), trial juror Amelia Franza, and childhood friend Barry Springer.

The centerpiece of the documentary was an interview of DeFeo by Dr. Steven Hoge, director of forensic psychiatry at Bellevue Hospital in New York City. Still housed at Green Haven, DeFeo spoke about violent fights with his father and his heavy drug use and drinking. Again, he recounted the "Dawn killed the younger siblings" version, this time with some new details. Describing the killings as more of a tragedy than a crime, DeFeo tended to blame Dawn for how the whole thing unfolded. He said he and Dawn had originally planned to kill their father in an automobile accident, but things got "out of hand" when Dawn insisted he be killed immediately.

In this telling, DeFeo gave Dawn the loaded rifle to kill their father, but when she hesitated he took it from her and killed him himself. When his mother awakened and reached for a handgun kept under her pillow, he had to shoot her. Leaving the house "in a fog," he returned to find Allison, Marc, and John dead. After a struggle for the rifle, he killed Dawn.

When Hoge suggested that DeFeo had killed the entire family, DeFeo began to argue with him and insisted he would not change his story and admit to killing the younger siblings. DeFeo claimed

 THOMAS M. STARK

that Dawn's killing was, at the most, manslaughter (reckless homicide). During the program, officer Della Penna explained that contrary to DeFeo's claim, the gunpowder residue found on Dawn's nightgown did not show that she fired the rifle. Instead, it came from the muzzle being close to her when she was shot.

Hoge, speaking from his office after the interview, explained that in his opinion as a psychiatrist, DeFeo's various versions of the killings were meant to elicit sympathy from different audiences. He also believed, based on his interview, that DeFeo did kill all six family members and was so mentally disturbed by the killings of Allison, Marc, and John that he could not bring himself to admit these killings. Because of this he wanted to blame Dawn. "I didn't find anything credible about the Dawn story," Hoge said. "What was most believable was DeFeo's emotional honesty, how he became visibly uncomfortable when he talked about his three young siblings. This made me believe that he had actually killed them." The DeFeo documentary was telecast by the A&E network several times after its initial showing.

THE MANY MRS. DEFEOS

Between 1989 and 2004, DeFeo married in prison three times and divorced twice. In January 1985 DeFeo, at the time an inmate at Auburn State Prison in Auburn, New York, met Geraldine Gates, the woman he would claim in court filings five year later was his wife in 1974. A married woman with a ten-year-old daughter, she was on parole after serving a prison sentence for a fraudulent check scheme. Under prison rules, as a parolee, she was not allowed to visit DeFeo.

To solve this problem, DeFeo paid a correction officer's wife $200 to pose as "Geraldine DeFeo" and obtain an identification card from the Sheriff's office in nearby Cayuga County. During their visits, DeFeo and Gates concocted the story that they had married in New Jersey in

1974 and had a daughter born that summer (passing off Gates's daughter as DeFeo's child). Their scheme was to obtain money from the Ronald DeFeo Sr. and Louise DeFeo estates. A court had ruled that if DeFeo was married and had a child when he was arrested for the murders, his child had a valid claim against the estates. There was nothing in my research indicating that this scheme ever resulted in any payments from the estates.

In 1989, while DeFeo was an inmate at Sullivan Correctional Facility, DeFeo and Gates went through a marriage ceremony performed by the Catholic chaplain. Gates used a fictitious maiden name and indicated on the marriage transcript that it was her first marriage. DeFeo and Gates knew that this marriage was bigamous; she was married to Gerald Gates at the time. The reason for this marriage ceremony is not clear, but I believe it may have been done to permit Gates (now known as DeFeo's wife as a result of the ceremony) to have conjugal visits with DeFeo. All of the New York State maximum security prisons house trailers inside the walls, each containing a living room, bedroom, kitchen and bath to accommodate inmates and their spouses. To have a conjugal visit, an inmate applies to the Department of Corrections in Albany, identifying his wife and providing an address and proof of marriage. DeFeo's 1989 marriage certificate could provide such proof.

The inmate and spouse are given privacy in the trailer during the conjugal visits, which generally last twenty-four hours. Most wives bring special food to prepare in the trailer kitchen. New York is one of seven states offering a conjugal-visit program. These special visits are not limited to wives (though such visits largely predominate). As the official name "Family Reunion Program" implies, inmates are permitted to have one of their parents (usually the mother) utilize them.

After the 1992 Supreme Court Article 440 hearing in which DeFeo's claim of a 1974 marriage to Gates was exposed as false (Gates's sworn statements to the contrary didn't help), DeFeo decided to terminate the 1989 bigamous marriage. He brought a divorce action in the Supreme Court in the judicial district where the prison was located, drafting his own summons and complaint. New York law provides only limited

     THOMAS M. STARK

grounds for divorce, one being abandonment by the other spouse for one year or more prior to the commencement of the divorce action. In his divorce complaint, DeFeo claimed that Gates, while visiting him in 1991, said she would not be returning because she no longer loved him and thereafter refused to visit or communicate with him. This situation had continued for more than one year. Gates failed to appear or oppose the divorce action, and on October 18, 1993, the divorce was granted.

According to Ric Osuna's 2003 book concerning the DeFeo family murders entitled *The Night the DeFeos Died*, when Osuna was doing research for his publication in 2000 he was contacted by a woman calling herself Geraldine DeFeo, who claimed to be the former wife of Ronald DeFeo. While he was initially skeptical of her claim, he said he later became convinced that she was telling the truth.

Osuna said she told him that she had married DeFeo in 1970—four years before the murders—and given birth to their daughter in the summer of 1974. She shared considerable details about first meeting DeFeo and her cordial relations with the DeFeo and Brigante families. Recounting what DeFeo had told her of how the murders took place, she said that Dawn, DeFeo's friend Bobby Kelske, and another man were involved with DeFeo in the killings. After investigating what he had been told by the woman he believed was DeFeo's former wife, Osuna incorporated the material into his book. Geraldine DeFeo (who in fact was Geraldine Gates) authored the foreword in *The Night the DeFeos Died*, in which she explained why she was coming forward and her belief that the book would finally reveal the true facts of the DeFeo murders.

DeFeo sued Osuna and the book's publisher in federal court in Manhattan, claiming the book was not a true story and defamed him. The district judge dismissed the case, stating that DeFeo's reputation was already tarnished and could not be further tarnished. DeFeo's defamation suit against Geraldine Gates in the New York State Supreme Court was dismissed for the same reason. (Gates reportedly died in 2015.)

After his 1993 divorce from Gates, DeFeo remained unmarried for only six months, according to a website he later ran. In April 1994 he married Barbara Puco, and this marriage lasted five years until 1999, when she divorced DeFeo to marry the man she was then living with. DeFeo's third marriage was to Tracey Lynn on April 28, 2004. (One wonders why some women are apparently attracted to a middle-aged convicted murderer serving six life sentences, but as the saying goes, "Love is blind.")

In 2005 Ronald and Tracey DeFeo created two websites concerning his convictions and related matters: "The Night Exposed" and "The Injustices of Amityville." These sister sites, which were linked to each other, contained extensive commentary about the murder case and DeFeo's assertions that police, prosecutorial, and judicial corruption took place. In online posts, DeFeo described his version of the events of November 1974 in which Dawn killed his younger siblings. This time he made no mention of him killing Dawn. He repeated his police brutality allegations (the details embellished beyond his pretrial testimony), claimed that the police made up the Mazzeo version of the killings (the allegedly mob-connected friend of his father's that DeFeo fingered in his first statement to the police), and denied that he confessed to the police. He claimed Weber told him to falsely testify that his family was plotting to kill him and that he shot them in self-defense. Expressing remorse for the killings, he wrote that he wished none of this had ever happened.

The websites sold T-shirts, sweatshirts, posters, and coffee mugs, the graphic imprinted on each a reproduction of DeFeo's color painting of the Amityville house. There was also a link to a companion site memorializing the six murder victims, with no mention of how each died, only the date of death and the location of their graves. Visitors to this site could post their own condolences and order sympathy cards.

Both DeFeo websites announced that a new book concerning the DeFeo case was being authored by Steven Morris and would be entitled *Ronnie DeFeo* and subtitled *The True Story of the Man Who Inspired the Amityville Horror Myth*. The announcement stated that DeFeo would disclose all the facts of what had really happened and which he claimed have been suppressed. No publication date was given. If and when published, it should be an interesting read!

EPILOGUE

The DeFeo family murders are remembered today principally by Long Islanders alive in the 1970s and 1980s and by those who had a role in Ronald DeFeo's prosecution. The murders remain unique in that DeFeo's motive to kill his entire family has never been clearly established in the more than 40 years since the events occurred. At DeFeo's trial there was no legal requirement that the district attorney establish his motive in order for him to be convicted of the murders. It was only legally required that his intent (his conscious objective) to kill each victim be established beyond a reasonable doubt in order to convict him of the six murders, regardless of his motive.

Assistant District Attorney Sullivan argued to the jury that DeFeo's motive to kill was his father's discovery that he had stolen a large sum of money that his father had stashed in the hidden cash box. In his argument, Sullivan relied on the testimony of the jail inmate John Kramer, who said DeFeo had told him this story, and the fact that after the murders the cash box found by the police was empty and wiped clean of fingerprints.

To my mind, this was hardly convincing proof of DeFeo's motive. Despite an extensive search, no money was found among DeFeo's personal possessions or concealed in places where he might have hidden it. After DeFeo was arrested, some people said that in addition to the cash, DeFeo had also stolen the family jewelry, but all the jewelry was later found in his parents' safe deposit box.

DeFeo's statements about his motive were inconsistent, depending on the particular version of the killings he was describing. In a recent version, he claimed that he killed his father so that Dawn could leave the household and live with her boyfriend in Florida and DeFeo could leave and take off with his girlfriend. He killed his mother, he asserted, to defend himself when she reached for a handgun kept somewhere in her bed.

In several of his statements, DeFeo claimed that during his short absence from the house Dawn fired three lethally accurate rifle shots killing Allison, Marc, and John, and that he then killed Dawn in a rage to punish her for killing the children. This version is totally unbelievable. To claim that an eighteen-year-old girl, with no experience in firing a high-powered lever-action hunting rifle, could kill three others with three fatal shots fired in a period of seconds in dimly lit bedrooms is to me preposterous.

For readers who seek further knowledge of the murders, I recommend the Sullivan/Aronson book, *High Hopes: The Amityville Murders*, which recounts the details of Sullivan's pretrial preparation and trial strategy. It is an interesting story of the prosecutor's challenges and decisions in the case. There's no shortage of books espousing more far-out theories about the murders. Hans Holzer's book, *Murder in Amityville*, may be of particular interest to those who believe in the power of a medium to reach and communicate with spirits of the dead, and that such spirits can influence the activity of the living. Ric Osuna's book, *The Night the DeFeos Died: Reinvestigating the Amityville Murders*, tells a version of the DeFeo family murders largely based upon Geraldine Gates's story and Osuna's examination of the public records of the case.

For those who are interested in the haunted house tale that followed the murders, I recommend reading the Lutzes' story in *The Amityville Horror: A True Story*, a twenty-eight-day diary of the psychic events allegedly occurring in the DeFeo house. For the details of the investigation and exposure of the hoax, I suggest the Kaplan book, *The Amityville Horror Conspiracy*. It describes the conspiracy between DeFeo's lawyer, William Weber, and George Lutz to create the haunted house story—and its ultimate public exposure as a hoax by Weber himself.

PART 2

The Scorned Woman
The Benjamin Mattana Murder
April 28, 1976

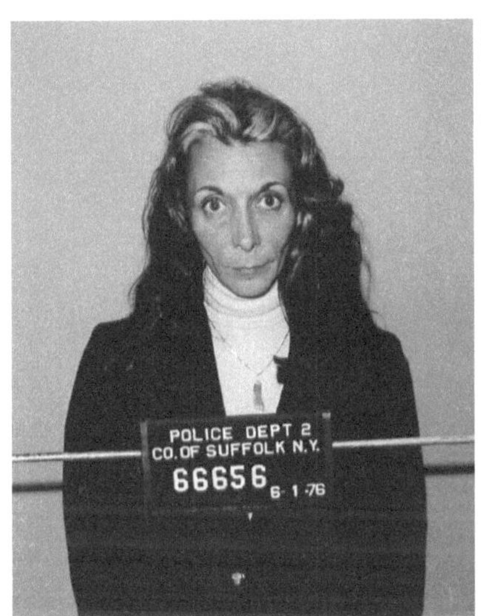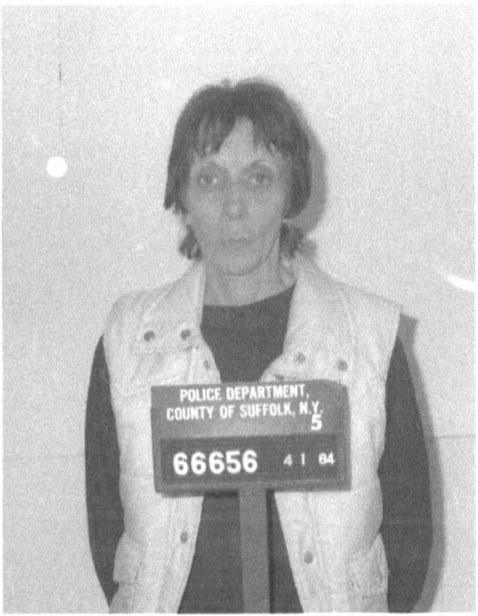

Frances Victoria Ardito, arrested on June 1, 1976, for conspiring
to kidnap and murder her boyfriend, and arrested again
on April 1, 1984, after fleeing a mental hospital

THE UNFAITHFUL PARAMOUR

Frances Victoria Morea was born in Flushing, New York, on December 9, 1936, the younger daughter of Victor N. Morea, a hairdresser, and Frances Bruno Morea. She attended Catholic elementary and high schools and started secretarial school. Leaving school at nineteen, she married Gerald Ardito, a Fordham University student. The young bride—known to all as Vikki—and her husband lived with her parents until his graduation from Fordham. He went into the packaging industry, becoming very successful. By age thirty-three, Ardito was a self-made millionaire, owning his own company in Long Island City.

After living in several Queens County apartments, Vikki and Gerald Ardito moved to a large house in Old Westbury, Long Island. Between 1957 and 1971, they had five children and lived luxuriously, with live-in maids and gardeners. Yet amid all this good fortune, tragedy struck the family. Victor, the middle child, died as an infant in 1961 after falling from his stroller and striking his head.

In the wake of this terrible accident, Vikki Ardito took up motorcycle riding as a hobby. Her husband purchased an automobile service station, which Ardito operated on her own, becoming a skilled mechanic. After the station was sold, she engaged in various charitable activities—and acquired and trained young chimpanzees. Her first chimp, named Tuff Guy, was the subject of a small item in the *Daily News* in 1970 and again appeared in the paper in 1971, when Ardito brought him into New York City on the Long Island Rail Road. She took the animals to children's hospitals and other institutions on Long Island, where the chimps performed for the patients and Ardito handed out "Tuff Guy" and "Tuff Gal" t-shirts. When the chimps grew too large to accompany Ardito, they were donated to zoos.

Although Ardito's charitable activities brought her public attention and admiration, her home life was not happy. Her husband was an alcoholic with a ferocious temper, she later maintained, and there were many arguments and even violence at times. Ardito said he "fooled around." With her husband spending long hours at his business, Ardito had to manage the children alone. Through her motorcycling, Ardito met Benjamin Mattana Jr., nearly nine years younger than she and unmarried. He was the owner and proprietor of the Nassau Harley-Davidson motorcycle dealership in Lynbrook, Long Island. Ardito purchased several motorcycles there and began to ride with Mattana. When Ardito was hospitalized after injuring her foot and losing two toes in a motorcycle accident, Mattana came to see her daily, while her husband did not visit at all.

In 1974 Ardito began a relationship with Mattana and moved out of the Old Westbury house to live with him. Gerald Ardito did not contest his wife's separation and agreed to provide her with support payments. Mattana and Ardito purchased a ranch house at 107 Browns Road in Lloyd Harbor, Long Island. Ardito sold her jewelry and used the proceeds to extensively renovate the house. She opened a plant store in nearby Huntington, which she named Vikki's Plantique. Her teenaged children maintained a close relationship with her and often visited the Lloyd Harbor house. In 1975 Ardito met another motorcycle rider, nineteen-year-old Sebastian Ventimiglia of South Ozone Park, Queens, and began to ride with him. At the behest of Gerald Ardito, Ventimiglia, who went by "Ben" or "Benny," began to teach Ardito's son Jed karate at the Old Westbury house.

Ardito's relationship with Mattana began to deteriorate in early 1976. He had become an excessive drug user and had introduced Ardito's daughter Geraldine (known as Deena) to illegal drugs. He had made no effort to reimburse Ardito for the considerable sum she had spent to renovate the Lloyd Harbor house, which was owned in his name. Mattana had also become involved with another woman much younger than Ardito, and she feared that at age thirty-nine she was losing her physical attractiveness.

She could have moved out and returned to her husband or found another place to live, perhaps in the same community as her plant store. (In fact, she did consult a real estate agent and looked at nearby rentals.) Instead, she made a horrendous decision: Benjamin Mattana should be killed. She began to consider how this might be accomplished—perhaps a motorcycle "accident" or an overdose of cocaine.

John Dellacona Jr., known to all as "Junior," had worked for Ardito at her service station years before. The twenty-four-year-old had kept in touch over the years and knew she was living with Mattana in Lloyd Harbor. Now married and living in Brooklyn, he worked at Creedmoor State Hospital in Queens Village. In March 1976 he called Ardito seeking to borrow $500, and she asked him to come out to her plant store in Huntington. There they talked over old times, and she told him of her troubled relationship with Mattana and that she was thinking of killing him or having him killed. He was shocked by her remark and could not believe she was serious. She agreed to lend Dellacona the money but said that it would take some time to arrange.

After leaving the store, Dellacona followed Ardito to the Lloyd Harbor house, where she gave him a tour. Ardito again brought up the subject of having Mattana killed and offered Dellacona $10,000 to help. She told him that she had told Gerald Ardito of her plan to kill Mattana, and he did not want to become involved. Given that, she'd decided to make the arrangements herself. Dellacona now believed that Ardito was serious and told her that he wanted no part of it. Saying he would see her again in several weeks, he left for Brooklyn.

James Pape, a teenage neighbor on Browns Road, had developed a "substitute mother" fixation on Ardito and become a frequent visitor when he wasn't in school. He became friendly with her teenage children when they visited Ardito at Lloyd Harbor and also got to know Ventimiglia, who often came on his motorcycle to ride with Ardito. Before Pape went to Florida with his family on April 10, 1976, during Easter vacation, Ardito confided in him, telling him of her plan to kill

Mattana by a drug overdose or have him killed at the motorcycle shop. She told Pape to keep her plan secret.

After his return from Florida on April 20, Pape was again at Ardito's house, and on this occasion he overheard a conversation between Ardito and Ventimiglia. She told Ventimiglia about her plan to have Mattana killed at the motorcycle shop, and he said he could do the job and make it appear that it happened during a robbery. If Pape had told his parents and the police what he now knew of Ardito's plan, the murder probably could have been prevented. Ventimiglia had an extensive criminal record of robberies in New York City, and Pape's mention of his involvement to the police would have given credence to his story and caused quick action by the authorities. Pape's misplaced loyalty to Ardito kept him from speaking.

On April 21, Dellacona visited Ardito at her house in Lloyd Harbor, and she told him that she had arranged for Mattana's murder at the motorcycle shop by a friend, Ben Ventimiglia. Adding that she didn't completely trust Ventimiglia, she said she wanted Dellacona to be present at the murder to "make sure it's done right." Dellacona was adamant in his continued refusal to be involved in Ardito's plan.

On April 24, Ardito inexplicably told two of her employees at the plant store, Jamie Kurzweil and Ann Chiechi, that she was going to have Mattana killed. Both knew of Ardito's troubled relationship with Mattana and thought she was just musing. Neither believed she was serious, and they put her remark out of their minds.

A VIOLENT END

Ventimiglia went ahead with his preparation. He brought a friend, sixteen-year-old Mario Russo of Brooklyn, into the murder plot. Russo possessed an illegal handgun that would be used to shoot and kill Mattana. Ventimiglia and Russo drove to Lloyd Harbor on the afternoon of April 27 and met Ardito at her house. They agreed that the murder would take place that evening and that the three of them would meet at a location in Nassau County near Lynbrook at a time when Mattana would be working at the motorcycle shop. Ardito called Dellacona at Creedmoor hospital and asked him to meet her that evening at 7:30 at Exit 19 of the Southern State Parkway (Peninsula Boulevard). She also called Pape to tell him that she was meeting Ventimiglia that evening and ask him to go to her house "to cover for her."

Dellacona drove to the meeting place expecting that Ardito had the money she was lending him and was going to give it to him. Ardito arrived and, to Dellacona's surprise, Ventimiglia and Russo showed up in a Lincoln driven by Ventimiglia's brother. The three cars parked at a nearby bowling alley, and Ardito and Dellacona got into the Lincoln. Russo handed Ventimiglia, who had on driving gloves, a 9 mm semiautomatic blue steel pistol, and Dellacona, now realizing what was happening, said he wanted out. Ventimiglia said they needed a car and driver—he was staying. Ardito said Dellacona could be trusted, and he became an unwilling accomplice.

All four moved to Dellacona's car, and Ventimiglia's brother left in the Lincoln. Leaving Russo and Dellacona in the parked car, Ardito and Ventimiglia drove in her car to Mattana's motorcycle shop in Lynbrook, arriving at about 8:00 p.m. They found the shop still open, with several customers and Mattana in the showroom and the manager in the office. Ventimiglia said the place was too busy to go ahead with the murder there, and he and Ardito returned to the bowling alley parking lot, where they rejoined Russo and Dellacona.

Rather than wait awhile and return to the motorcycle shop, it was decided that Mattana would be killed when he returned to the Lloyd Harbor house after closing the shop. Leaving in both cars, with Ventimiglia and Russo in Dellacona's car, they drove to Huntington, where they left Dellacona's car in a parking lot. All four got into Ardito's car and drove to the Lloyd Harbor house, arriving at 9:30 p.m. Pape was at the house and, seeing the pistol in Ventimiglia's belt, asked what was going on. Ardito said the boy could be trusted. Still, Ventimiglia threatened to shoot him if he said anything.

After Ardito declared she did not want Mattana killed in the house, Ventimiglia said he and Russo had a spot near the Belt Parkway in Queens where Mattana could be killed and the body would not be discovered for some time. Dellacona later testified that Ventimiglia and Russo discussed having previously dumped bodies at the site (what they called "their spot"). According to Dellacona, when asked if they'd done this before, Ventimiglia responded, "Yeah, we did it before." It was then agreed that after Mattana came home and retired for the night, he would be awakened by Ventimiglia and Russo, forcibly abducted at gunpoint, driven in Dellacona's car to the spot in Queens, and killed.

The plan was unexpectedly delayed when Mattana called Ardito from the motorcycle shop. He'd be stopping home and picking her up to go to a friend's house in Northport to watch wrestling on television. When Mattana briefly stopped at the house about 10:30 p.m. along with a friend, Ventimiglia, Russo and Dellacona hid in a rear bedroom until the couple left. Pape was still at the house, and Mattana told him to find the dog and tie him up for the night. Pape stayed around for a while, then headed home at 11:00 p.m. He now knew, after hearing the plan discussed at the house, that Mattana's abduction and murder were going to take place later that night. He probably could have prevented the crimes by speaking to his parents and the police. But Ventimiglia had warned Pape to stay quiet or he'd "blow his brains out," and the teenager did as he was told.

Ardito and Mattana came home shortly after midnight, still with their friend Mark Ambers, who sat around talking to Ardito and Mattana until 1:15 am. Ventimiglia, Russo, and Dellacona were hiding in the rear bedroom, having been alerted by a telephone ring signal from Ardito. They remained there until Ardito and Mattana had gone to bed in the master bedroom. After waiting awhile, Ventimiglia and Russo burst into the bedroom, with Ventimiglia wearing an ape mask that he had found in the house. Ventimiglia began to beat Mattana in the face with the pistol and demanded money. Ardito feigned surprise and attempted to "protect" Mattana from the assault by moving her body between him and Ventimiglia to "take" the blows. At the trial, the prosecutor made a point of how Ardito posed as the victim, "even cradling Mattana's bloody head after he was pistol-whipped," he said.

Ardito said there was no money in the house, and Ventimiglia demanded the keys to the motorcycle shop and the combination to the safe. Mattana said the manager had the keys, and Ventimiglia ordered Mattana to tell Ardito the combination, which she wrote down on a motor vehicle ID form from her purse.

Ventimiglia told Russo to have Ardito drive him to the shop in Lynbrook, open the safe, remove any money and come back. Ardito "protested" being forced to leave with Russo, but once outside she and Russo drove to the manager's house, where she obtained the keys on a pretext of needing papers Mattana wanted and continued on to the shop. At this point, it was about 3:00 a.m. Once inside, Ardito opened the office safe while Russo held the form and read the combination to her. Russo removed a bag from the safe containing $2,376 and in doing so dropped the form with the combination to the floor, where it remained after they left the shop. They drove to Huntington, where Russo picked up Dellacona's car, and both cars were driven to the Lloyd Harbor house.

Ventimiglia had held Mattana at gunpoint during Ardito and Russo's absence, and when they returned Ardito said she had been unable to open the safe. Ventimiglia knew however from Russo's nod to him that the safe had been opened and the money stolen. He ordered Mattana to get dressed and told him he would be taken to the shop to get the safe open. Mattana was blindfolded, taken to Dellacona's car and placed in the rear seat.

While all these events were occurring, Dellacona remained in the house, observing what was taking place and hearing the conversations. He made no effort to leave when Ventimiglia was holding Mattana at gunpoint while Ardito and Russo were at the motorcycle shop, fearful of being shot by Ventimiglia if he attempted to do so. The stolen money was transferred to Dellacona's car, and, with Ventimiglia holding Mattana at gunpoint in the rear seat while Russo rode in the front seat, Dellacona drove, following Ventimiglia and Russo's directions. By now, it was after 4:00 a.m.

After they had driven beyond the parkway exit for Lynbrook, Mattana realized he was not being taken to the motorcycle shop. Seeing that he was being abducted and probably being taken to be killed, he began to plead for his life, offering money to his captors to spare him. Ventimiglia scorned him, and Dellacona was directed to drive to Howard Beach in Queens. This community is located on the north shore of Jamaica Bay, and the populated area is surrounded by wetlands. As they arrived there at about dawn on April 28, Ventimiglia directed Dellacona to drive to a desolate area near the intersection of 160th Avenue and 80th Street, where a dirt road entered the wetlands about 250 feet from the nearest dwelling.

Dellacona drove a short distance down this road until Ventimiglia told him to stop. Mattana was taken from the car, still blindfolded, and Ventimiglia led him about seventy-five feet into the high reeds of the wetlands. There he fired five shots into Mattana, one bullet entering the head and brain, several entering the chest, and another entering the left forearm. Mattana fell backward onto the marshy ground. Death was instantaneous. Returning to the car, Ventimiglia told the others that Mattana was dead. Dellacona was directed to drive to Russo's home on Liberty Avenue in Ridgewood, where Ventimiglia gave the pistol to Russo and told him to get rid of it. Ventimiglia then had Dellacona drive to his home on 130th Place in South Ozone Park, where he took the bag of stolen money from the car and warned Dellacona not to tell anyone what had occurred. Leaving Ventimiglia at about 6:30 a.m., Dellacona drove home to Brooklyn.

THE PLOT UNRAVELS

After Mattana was taken from the house, Ardito did not yet know whether he had been killed. But she knew that Mattana's "kidnapping" would have to be reported to the police. In describing his "abduction," she would have to convince the police, the media and the public that a horrible crime had been committed in the upscale Village of Lloyd Harbor. Throughout an extensive police investigation, it would take a fair degree of acting ability to pose as a shocked victim hoping for Mattana's safe return. Years later, Mattana's father would bitterly recall Ardito coming to his house for a Sunday family dinner during this time and praying with them for their son's return.

At 5:17 a.m., she telephoned John Robertson, a friend and Suffolk County Police Officer, telling him that something had happened and asking him to come to the house. Robertson quickly dressed and drove to the Mattana house, where he found Ardito hysterical. She told him that earlier that morning four unknown men had entered the house, two of them armed, awakened her and Mattana and demanded money. Ardito said two of the men forced her to dress and accompany them to Mattana's motorcycle shop, where she opened the safe. After they removed the contents from the safe, they returned to Lloyd Harbor, where the four men forcibly abducted Mattana, took him from the house and drove away. Ardito also called Pape in the early morning hours, asking him to come over. Once there, she told him to call Mattana's father, then sent him out to buy cigarettes.

Robertson called the Lloyd Harbor Village police and the Suffolk County police, and officers quickly responded to the house. Ardito told them what had happened, but said she was not able to give them a detailed description of the intruders. Sobbing profusely, she said she was frantically worried over Mattana's safety. The detectives made a careful search of the house for clues as to the identity of the alleged kidnappers and found nothing. Receiving no word from the alleged kidnappers for twenty-four hours, the police notified the Federal Bureau of Investigation, and its agents joined the investigation. By May 5, the police had obtained telephone company records of all outgoing telephone calls made on April 26 and 27 from the Mattana house. These records showed the time of each call and the name and address of the subscriber to whom the call was made. Analysis of these calls became a part of the investigation into Mattana's disappearance.

Sebastian Ventimiglia came to the attention of the police when Officer Robertson told them that Ventimiglia rode his motorcycle with Ardito and was a frequent visitor at the Mattana house. The police visitor log showed that he visited Ardito at the house on May 7, after Mattana's disappearance. (It is interesting to speculate as to what went on between Ardito and Ventimiglia during that visit. Ardito had agreed to pay Ventimiglia for the murder of Mattana. It is unknown whether Ardito paid him on the afternoon of April 27, when he and Russo came to Lloyd Harbor, or at the post-murder May 7 visit, nearly under the eyes of the police!)

With knowledge of Ventimiglia's extensive criminal record and access to his probation department records in New York City, which contained details of his personal life in South Ozone Park, the police determined that three telephone calls made from the Mattana house during the late evening of April 27, before Mattana's disappearance, were to subscribers in Queens County who were Ventimiglia's close friends. Ventimiglia now became a suspect in Mattana's disappearance, but the police did not have probable cause for his arrest. Police also learned that the Brooklyn teenager Mario Russo had accompanied Ventimiglia on his visit to Ardito at the Mattana house on the afternoon of April 27.

On May 12, the police picked up Russo in Brooklyn for questioning. He willingly went with them to Suffolk County, where he was interrogated about Mattana's disappearance. He said he and Ventimiglia had visited Ardito at the Lloyd Harbor house on April 27 but had gone to Philadelphia right after the visit and only learned of Mattana's disappearance after their return. Being suspicious of what appeared to be a fabricated alibi, the police, with Russo's permission, took his fingerprints before bringing him back to Brooklyn.

On the morning after Mattana's disappearance, the police found the piece of paper with the combination to the motorcycle shop safe on the office floor, and police kept it because it had an unidentified fingerprint on it. This fingerprint was compared with Russo's fingerprints, and it matched his left thumb. The police now had evidence that Russo had possibly been present in the shop when the safe was opened, and he also became a suspect in the case.

The police also learned of James Pape's close friendship with Ardito and his constant presence at the Mattana house. He was questioned as to his knowledge of what may have occurred before Mattana's disappearance. Claiming he knew nothing, he lied to the police. By this time, he must have surmised that Mattana had been murdered by Ventimiglia as planned, but still fearing Ventimiglia, he kept quiet.

On May 26, a severely decomposed body was found in the wetlands near the shore of Jamaica Bay at Howard Beach. New York City police believed from the clothing that it might be Benjamin Mattana's body and notified the Suffolk County police, who responded to the scene. Positive identification was made by comparing fingerprints taken from the body with Mattana's fingerprint records and by comparing the body's teeth with Mattana's dental records.

An autopsy was performed at the New York City morgue. The skull had a single bullet entry hole behind the left ear, and there were several bullet entry-holes on the upper chest. A loose expended bullet was found in the brain cavity and another in the left forearm. Metallic fragments were found in the chest area, indicating that several bullets had passed through the chest. The shirt removed from the body had multiple bullet holes in it. The medical examiner certified that death was caused by bullet wounds of the brain and chest. He believed that death had occurred at least thirty days prior to the autopsy. The expended bullets found in the body were examined by a ballistics expert of the city police, who determined that both were 9 mm caliber.

The Suffolk County police learned that John Dellacona Jr., a.k.a. Junior, had visited Ardito at her plant store in Huntington and at the Mattana house several times before Mattana's disappearance, and they were interested in him because he had a minor criminal record years before. On May 29, they asked Ardito what she knew about Dellacona. She said she knew him but had not seen him for many years, and she could give them no information about him. After this response, which the police knew to be false, the police believed that Ardito had not been truthful in her earlier statements and suspected that she had been somehow involved in Mattana's disappearance.

Believing that Dellacona might know something about Mattana's disappearance and might cooperate in the investigation, the police went to his home in Brooklyn very early on the morning of June 1. Dellacona agreed to go with the officers to the police precinct in Huntington. There he was interrogated by an assistant district attorney with a court reporter and a detective present. Offering no reluctance, he told those present about his involvement in all the events of April 27 and 28. He recounted what happened in considerable detail, fully implicating Ardito, Ventimiglia, and Russo in the criminal conspiracy, the abduction of Mattana, and his intentional murder in the wetlands at Howard Beach. Admitting his own participation in the abduction, Dellacona agreed to cooperate in the prosecution of the trio. Later that morning he appeared before a grand jury and testified as to all the facts he had discussed earlier that day.

That afternoon the grand jury indicted Ardito, Ventimiglia, Russo, and Dellacona, charging them with criminal conspiracy, kidnapping, and both intentional and felony (kidnapping) murder. Ardito and Ventimiglia were arrested that evening. Early the following morning, June 2, Russo learned of his indictment and quickly left home to avoid imminent arrest, becoming a fugitive. His relatives insisted to the police that they did not know his whereabouts. Ardito was arraigned in County Court that same morning. As the *Daily News* described it, "Frances Victoria Ardito of Old Westbury bowed her head while her husband stood nearby with tears in his eyes as she pleaded innocent." She was released on bail.

Pape was questioned by the police in the presence of his parents on June 2. He was informed that Dellacona had told them that Pape was at the Mattana house on the evening of April 27 when he, Ardito,

          THOMAS M. STARK

Ventimiglia, and Russo had arrived, and that Pape was present when they discussed the abduction and murder of Mattana. Admitting to the police that he had lied when questioned after Mattana's disappearance, he now revealed everything: how Ardito told him in early April that she was going to have Mattana killed; his overhearing the conversation between Ardito and Ventimiglia on April 20; and what he had seen and heard at the house on the evening of April 27. He had not spoken up before April 27, he told the police, because he did not want to "hurt Vikki." After April 27, he kept quiet because he was afraid of Ventimiglia. Pape agreed to cooperate in the investigation and testify for the prosecution at trial.

A DEFENDANT INCAPACITATED

On August 31, the county administrative judge transferred the case from the County Court to the Criminal Term of the Supreme Court, where I was presiding. After the indictment, Ardito and Ventimiglia had both been represented by John J. Sutter of Mineola, Long Island, a prominent criminal defense attorney, who had been hired by Ardito's husband. By October, Sutter could no longer represent both Ardito and Ventimiglia due to a potential conflict of interest between the two. He was relieved from representing Ventimiglia and continued to represent Vikki Ardito, his fees still being paid by Gerald Ardito. Ventimiglia obtained new counsel.

On December 1, after six months as a fugitive, Mario Russo surrendered to the authorities. It was said at the time, and believed by many, that he surrendered after his family was threatened by mob-connected "enforcers" acting at the behest of Benjamin Mattana Sr., who bore great anger and animosity against the defendants over the senseless murder of his son.

A week later, on December 9, Ventimiglia and Russo's older brother, Andrew Russo, attempted the armed robbery of a movie theater in

Queens. When the crime was interrupted by New York City police officers, Ventimiglia took a hostage and engaged in a shootout with the officers. Arrested and disarmed, he was charged with attempted murder of a police officer. His bail in Suffolk County was revoked, and he was confined to jail.

Junior Dellacona sought a separate trial because he was raising the defense of duress. I ordered that he be tried after the joint trial of Ardito, Ventimiglia, and Russo was completed.

Between June and December 1976, the district attorney and the police continued the investigation of the Mattana murder case, in search of further evidence to support the charges. The principal trial witness would be Dellacona. He was charged as an accomplice in the commission of the crimes, and a special rule of evidence would apply on trial. A person may not be convicted upon the testimony of an accomplice unsupported by corroborative evidence tending to connect the defendant with the commission of the crime. Therefore, if Ardito, Ventimiglia, and Russo were to be convicted, the district attorney had to present evidence, separate and apart from Dellacona's testimony, that connected the three with the conspiracy, kidnapping, and murder.

The pretrial investigation did produce such evidence. The police learned that Ardito had told her two plant store employees that she was going to kill Mattana. Pape's potential testimony linked all three defendants with the crimes. Russo's fingerprint on the form containing the office safe combination connected him with the commission of the crimes. An investigation of Ventimiglia's friends and acquaintances identified three witnesses whose potential testimony connected him to the crimes by reason of his self-incriminatory statements.

Shortly after the murder, Ventimiglia told a drug dealer, Michael Oakley, "I just wasted a dude and dumped a body in Howard Beach." He also asked Oakley to "alibi" him "as being in Philadelphia for the last couple of days," telling Oakley he would read about the reason for the alibi in the papers. Shortly before the crimes, Ventimiglia told another drug dealer, Jerry Tedeschi, to whom he owed money, that he should "not worry about it—something big was going down, and you will read about it in the paper."

Ventimiglia was engaged to be married to Anna Marie Pugliesi of South Ozone Park. In the late afternoon of April 27, 1976, Ventimiglia told her that he, his brother, and Mario Russo were going to Philadelphia that evening and would be back the next day. If anyone, including the police, were to ask her about their whereabouts, that is what she should say. Shortly after the murder, he said to Pugliesi, "I shot someone and don't know why I did it. I was the only one who had the guts to shoot him." Sometime about the middle of May, Ventimiglia told Pugliesi that a person named Junior was there at the time of the murder "as a witness to see the murder was done." He also told her that he and Russo had gotten money that they split up the night of the murder, and they were supposed to get more.

Oakley, Tedeshi, and Pugliesi, as well as plant store employees Jamie Kurzweil and Ann Chiechi and the teenage James Pape, were all scheduled to testify for the prosecution on trial. Ventimiglia and Russo were represented by separate attorneys. I do not know whether these attorneys' fees were being paid by Gerald Ardito or by someone else. He continued to pay Vikki Ardito's attorney and other expenses throughout the trial. By this time, it was being reported that she was back with her husband and children in their Old Westbury home.

The trial commenced on January 25, 1977. The trial prosecutor was Gerard B. Sullivan, chief of the major offense bureau of the Suffolk County District Attorney's office. I told the jury panel that the trial was expected to last nine to ten weeks and entertained excuses from those unable to serve that length of time. I explained to them the charges made in the indictment and emphasized that the indictment was simply an accusation and not proof of anything. The four attorneys proceeded with jury selection, which took seven days, and each attorney then made opening statements to the jury.

Over the next month, Sullivan presented the district attorney's case, including the testimony of fifty-eight witnesses and the admission of seventy-one documentary and physical exhibits. Police officers from the various departments that were involved in the overall investigation, including the FBI agents, testified. Other witnesses included the medical examiner from the autopsy, a fingerprint identification expert, a dental identification expert, and a firearm ballistics expert.

Seven weeks into the trial, when the prosecution had nearly completed its case, Ardito failed to appear in court. When the trial session opened on Wednesday, March 9, her attorney, John Sutter, told me that she was in Mt. Sinai Hospital in New York City. I agreed to recess the trial for the rest of the day and told Sutter I wanted to hear from her doctor about her medical condition as soon as possible. I heard nothing that day or the following, and on Friday I told Sutter that without definitive word from Ardito's doctor, she must appear at the trial on Monday, March 14, or I would issue a warrant compelling her attendance.

When I entered the courtroom on Monday morning, Sutter said Ardito was present but lying on the floor, and he was unable to communicate with her. Two court officers assisted Ardito to the counsel table, where she sprawled on the surface, still wearing her hospital gown and robe. She still was uncommunicative when Sutter and I spoke to her. I revoked her bail, directed that she be examined by appropriate doctors to determine her mental and physical condition, and arranged for her confinement for the time being in Central Islip Psychiatric Center. The trial was recessed until her status was determined.

On March 15, she was examined by psychiatrists Dr. Harold Zolan and Dr. Samuel Rosenberg, whose written reports were sent to me the following day. Ardito did not respond to the questions by both doctors during their examinations and appeared to them to be haggard and disheveled, wringing her hands, rocking back and forth and frequently crying. Each gave a different diagnosis. Zolan's was "adjustment reaction of adult life," and Rosenberg's was "agitated depression." In both doctors' opinions, because of her condition she could not communicate with her attorney and was therefore incapable of assisting in her defense.

A hearing was conducted before me the following day. Both psychiatrists testified and were examined by Sutter and Sullivan. The district attorney had the burden of establishing by a preponderance

    THOMAS M. STARK

of the credible evidence that Ardito was not an incapacitated person. (The legal standard for a person's capacity is being mentally capable of understanding the charges and assisting in his or her defense.) Because Ardito had demonstrated her acting ability in initially convincing the investigating police back in April and for several weeks thereafter that Mattana had been forcibly abducted by unknown intruders, I was somewhat skeptical as to her present conduct. Was she feigning incapacity in order to obtain a mistrial and thus avoid what she now realized was certain conviction by the jury very shortly? Or had the certainty of an upcoming conviction so mentally disturbed her that she was actually unable to continue at this point to confer with her attorney?

At the time of Ardito's purported breakdown, the presentation of the district attorney's proof was 95 percent complete, and the evidence of her criminal conduct was overwhelming. I had serious misgivings about her mental condition. However, both psychiatrists expressed their belief that Ardito was not faking a mental illness and maintained those positions despite extensive cross-examination. In my oral decision, I found that the district attorney had not met his burden and that Ardito was an incapacitated person within the meaning of the law. I committed her to the custody of the state commissioner of mental hygiene for confinement in Mid-Hudson Forensic Psychiatric Center at upstate New Hampton, New York, for a period of one year. My order provided that if Ardito was later found to be no longer incapacitated, the court and the district attorney were to be notified.

I then declared a mistrial as to Vikki Ardito. When the jury was ultimately brought back into the courtroom after nearly a week's absence, I explained that Ardito was not present because of certain rulings I had made. I did not disclose to them what my rulings were or any of the events that had taken place in court during the past week. The proceedings leading up to Ardito's mistrial had been widely reported in the media—"Mrs. Ardito Called Fake. Bail Revoked," and "Slay Trial Is Interrupted. Mrs. Ardito Is Committed," were just two of the New York tabloid headlines—and I cautioned the jury not to read any such accounts.

COURTROOM CHEERS

The trial, now only involving Ventimiglia and Russo, continued until the district attorney completed his case on March 18. Neither Ventimiglia nor Russo presented any evidence in their defense, nor did either testify in his own behalf. Before the attorneys' closing arguments, I told the jury they must disregard particular testimony and exhibits that related solely to Ardito and could not consider them evidence against Ventimiglia and Russo. The attorneys' closing arguments to the jury extended over several days.

On March 29, by then in the tenth week of the trial, I instructed the jury as to the law applicable to the case in general and the specific charges in the indictment: criminal conspiracy, kidnapping and intentional murder. (The district attorney had agreed that the felony murder charge not be submitted.) Deliberations began after lunch and continued until evening, interrupted only for dinner. After an overnight stay at the local hotel and breakfast, deliberations resumed in the morning and continued all day, interrupted only for lunch and dinner. At 10:30 p.m., after deliberations totaling twelve hours over two days, verdicts of guilty as charged of all the crimes in the indictment were rendered against Ventimiglia and Russo. Both sat impassively as the verdicts were read. I discharged the jury after thanking them for their service in one of the longest and most complex criminal trials ever held in the county.

I fixed the sentence date and directed the required presentence investigation. When interviewed by the probation officer, Ventimiglia and Russo denied any guilt whatsoever, and their families refused to believe either was guilty. In the written report, Russo was described as a seventeen-year-old school dropout with no criminal record whose only employment was at his family's pizzeria in Brooklyn. The report described Ventimiglia, now twenty-one, as a high-school dropout with a poor school record and spotty employment record. Ventimiglia was an extensive drug user, and the report stated that he had had marijuana smuggled into the jail by a girlfriend and was suspected of planning a jail escape. His criminal record extended over three years and included charges of robbing fourteen Fotomat kiosks in Queens and Kings Counties (Brooklyn), resulting in three felony robbery convictions in Queens on January 31, 1975, and a conviction for larceny in Kings on February 11, 1975. Given concurrent sentences of probation on these convictions, he was still serving these sentences when he kidnapped and killed Mattana in April 1976.

The probation department recommended that I impose lengthy prison sentences on Ventimiglia and Russo. The sentencing proceedings were held on April 27, 1977 (coincidently one year to the day after the commission of the crimes). Neither Ventimiglia nor Russo made any statement to me when invited to do so except to deny their guilt. I sentenced Russo first. The sole mitigating factor I considered was that he was a youth with no criminal record. An aggravating factor was that he illegally possessed the pistol that was used to kill Mattana and disposed of it afterward. I extended a modicum of leniency by imposing a twenty-year minimum instead of the twenty-five years authorized on the kidnapping and murder counts. I pronounced three sentences on Russo as follows: eight and one-third years to twenty-five years on the criminal conspiracy conviction; twenty years to life on the kidnapping conviction; twenty years to life on the intentional murder conviction; and I directed that they be served concurrently. I directed him to be delivered to the upstate Elmira reception center where offenders younger than 18 were initially imprisoned.

I then sentenced Ventimiglia. There were no mitigating factors in his case, and because he was a second felony offender a sentence of imprisonment was mandatory, and the minimum sentence must be one-half the maximum. I pronounced three sentences on Ventimiglia as follows: twelve and one-half years to twenty-five years on the criminal conspiracy conviction; twenty-five years to life on the kidnapping conviction; and twenty-five years to life on the intentional murder conviction, all to be served concurrently. I directed him to be delivered to upstate Ossining State Prison, the reception center for all sentenced adult felons from Long Island and the New York metropolitan area. Prior to going upstate, Ventimiglia was taken to Southampton Town Court (the jail is located in that township) to dispose of the marijuana smuggling case and then to Queens County Supreme Court for disposition of the December 1976 theater robbery and police shootout case.

Benjamin Mattana Sr., father of the murder victim, had attended every session of the lengthy trial. He arranged for a group of sixty leather-jacketed motorcycle enthusiasts, all of whom had known or dealt with Benjamin Mattana Jr. at his Harley-Davidson dealership, to be bussed to Riverhead for the sentencing. They nearly filled the spectator seats in the courtroom. After I finished the sentencing session and was about to leave the bench, the group burst into loud cheering and applause as Ventimiglia and Russo were being handcuffed by the court officers so they could be taken from the courtroom. Ventimiglia turned toward them, smiled, and raised his wrist-bound arms in front of him as if he were a prizefighter.

The crowd's clamor turned to boos and obscene gestures. Despite my admonishments, I was unable to quell the disturbance, and it continued until Ventimiglia and Russo were completely out of the courtroom. "Courtroom Cheers Life Terms for Killers" was the headline the next day in the *Daily News*. Afterward, Mattana Sr. told reporters he was "more than satisfied with what [Ventimiglia] got. My only wish is that they punish him in jail," *Newsday* reported.

Russo was received at Elmira on May 4, 1977, and became state inmate number 77B0720. In Queens County, Ventimiglia pled guilty to robbery first degree in the theater crime and was sentenced as a second felony offender and probation violator to a lengthy prison term. His codefendant, Andrew Russo, the twenty-year-old brother of Mario Russo, pled guilty to robbery second degree and was sentenced to two and one-third years to seven years. Ventimiglia was received at Ossining on July 14, 1977, and became state inmate number 77A2360.

Junior Dellacona waived a jury and was tried by State Supreme Court Justice Lawrence J. Bracken several months after Ventimiglia's sentencing. As noted, Dellacona raised the defense of duress to all the charges. If established, this defense requires an acquittal. Dellacona admitted his participation in Mattana's abduction but claimed he was forced to do so by Ventimiglia's threats to shoot him if he did not comply with the directions to first drive his car to Huntington and subsequently drive the abducted Mattana, Ventimiglia, and Russo to the location where Mattana was murdered. Ventimiglia "threatened to blow a hole in my head" if he refused, Dellacona said. At the site of the murder, he testified, "I was afraid they would kill me or come after my family." The district attorney did not attempt to impeach Dellacona's claim of duress. His testimony had been a major factor in Ventimiglia and Russo's convictions at trial, and he was owed a benefit. Judge Bracken found Dellacona not guilty of all the charges.

Ventimiglia and Russo appealed their convictions to the Appellate Division of the Supreme Court in Brooklyn. On January 21, 1980, four justices of that court affirmed the convictions without an opinion. The pair appealed that court's decision to the New York Court of Appeals in Albany, the state's highest court. On March 31, 1981, the seven judges of that court in a lengthy opinion affirmed the Appellate Division's decision upholding the convictions.

In an interesting side note, the Court of Appeals, in rendering its opinion, established the necessity of a pretrial hearing as to the admissibility of uncharged evidence of a crime, if it was to be offered by the prosecution (in this case, Ventimiglia and Russo's discussion of having previously dumped bodies in Howard Beach). These hearings, when they are now held, are called "Ventimiglia hearings."

After Russo's appeals were concluded, I was contacted by a person claiming to represent him and was asked to resentence Russo without a minimum period of imprisonment. He would then be immediately released from prison and deported as an undocumented alien. I told this person that I had no resentencing authority and that even if I did I would not use it in Russo's case.

In January 1987 Russo made a further effort to end his imprisonment. Having served half of his minimum twenty years (a prerequisite), he asked Governor Mario Cuomo to grant him executive clemency (an opportunity for early parole release). I was asked by the governor's counsel for my recommendation on the application. I submitted a lengthy letter describing Russo's complicity and participation in Mattana's abduction and brutal murder as the reasons he should not be granted clemency. Mattana's father and the district attorney also objected to Russo's application, and the governor did not act on the request.

THE SIX-YEAR RUSE

Vikki Ardito was admitted to Mid-Hudson Forensic Psychiatric Center on March 24, 1977. Mid-Hudson is a secure hospital for the confinement of criminal defendants from all parts of the state who have been determined by a court to be mentally incapacitated for purposes of trial, as well as criminal defendants who have been found by a court or jury to be legally insane. She was an evasive and uncooperative patient, claiming not to know the events and reasons leading to her hospitalization, and she was completely unwilling to discuss the criminal charges against her or even acknowledge the existence of these charges. Treated with antipsychotic drugs during the early months of her confinement, her mental condition appeared improved, but her claimed amnesia of her criminal situation continued.

After eleven months at Mid-Hudson, Ardito was transferred to South Beach Psychiatric Center on Staten Island. South Beach is a nonsecure, intermediate-level mental hospital serving New York City and area residents as inpatients and outpatients. At the time there was speculation about the actual reason for Ardito's transfer. She was a criminal status patient, and the great majority of those at South Beach were civil status. Many believed that her husband, through his political connections, had arranged the transfer to greatly shorten the distance family members had to travel to visit Ardito. South Beach had more comfortable accommodations, with a landscaped campus overlooking the waters of Lower New York Bay.

In March 1978 the South Beach director, stating that Ardito

continued to be mentally incapacitated, applied for a further one-year retention order. The district attorney and Ardito's new attorney, James LaRossa, were notified, and both sought a court hearing on the application (LaRossa later became famous for representing several New York mob bosses, among other notables). Ardito was transferred to Central Islip Psychiatric Center on Long Island so she could attend the hearing. All of her progress notes and clinical summaries from Mid-Hudson, South Beach, and Central Islip were sent to me, along with the written reports of the psychiatrists, psychologists, and psychiatric social workers who had attended Ardito at the three hospitals since March 1977. Prior to the hearing, Ardito was examined by Dr. Harold Zolan at the request of the district attorney. He was one of the two psychiatrists who had examined Ardito during trial and found her incapacitated at that time.

The hearing was conducted at Riverhead in a number of sessions during the next several weeks. The South Beach director was represented by an assistant state attorney general, and it was his burden to establish that Ardito continued to be mentally incapacitated. Three staff psychiatrists from the hospitals testified. Each said Ardito was mentally ill but differed in their diagnosis. A clinical psychologist testified that in his opinion Ardito was not "neurologically depressed" but was "situationally depressed," that is, she could cooperate in her criminal defense if she wanted to, but he believed she did not want to.

Zolan testified that Ardito had recovered from the condition he had diagnosed during trial and was no longer an incapacitated person. He believed that the different diagnoses of mental disease of the staff psychiatrists were not valid. In his opinion, Ardito was now feigning mental illness. Her appearance and conduct were all part of an act.

I wanted Ardito to be examined by a state psychiatrist who was not affiliated with the three hospitals where Ardito had been confined and treated, and one was designated by the commissioner of mental hygiene. He examined Ardito in the hospital and testified when the hearing was resumed. Finding her to be mentally ill and incapacitated, he thought she could not be feigning symptoms. At the end of the hearing, I rendered an oral decision finding that the attorney general had established to my satisfaction that Ardito continued to be an incapacitated person and ordered her retention for one year.

Even though I respected the opinion of Zolan, I found it hard to believe that Ardito had successfully faked the symptoms of each of the mental diseases diagnosed during the past sixteen months. During the following five years, I was not called upon to decide the issue of whether Ardito continued to be an incapacitated person, because no interested party raised the issue. In 1979 and 1981 the attorney general, district attorney, and Ardito's attorney stipulated in open court that Ardito remained incapacitated, and no hearing was requested. I was required by law after each stipulation to order her continued retention by the commissioner for a two-year period, and she remained confined in South Beach.

In the spring of 1980, Gerald Ardito brought an action for divorce against Vikki Ardito. She did not oppose the action, and the divorce was granted. The hospital records note that the divorce did not seem to affect Ardito's mental condition. Gerald Ardito remarried, and he and the two youngest children continued to reside in Old Westbury. Between November 1981 and September 1982 Ardito was able to obtain weekend passes from South Beach, which allowed her to leave the hospital grounds and visit her sister on Long Island. During several of these weekends, she was seen motorcycle riding in the Huntington area. She apparently convinced the person who issued the passes that she was a civil status patient entitled to leave. When the facility finally realized that she was a criminal status patient not entitled to passes, the practice was stopped, and an internal investigation ensued.

During Ardito's 1981-1983 retention period, the staff psychiatrists and psychologists at South Beach concluded that Ardito's mental condition was not improving and that she would not be able to attain the legal capacity to stand trial in the foreseeable future. Because of this conclusion, they recommended to the hospital director that Ardito's status be converted from criminal to civil pursuant to the mandate of a United States Supreme Court decision entitled *Jackson v. Indiana*. This case,

     THOMAS M. STARK

applicable nationwide, holds that a state may not continue to confine an incapacitated criminal defendant indefinitely in a criminal status, but after a reasonable length of time must hold a hearing to determine whether such defendant should be converted to civil status. A civil status patient has less stringent release standards and more personal privileges than one confined in the same institution under criminal status.

In late 1982 the South Beach director brought a proceeding in the Richmond County (Staten Island) Supreme Court for a *Jackson* hearing concerning Ardito's status. The Suffolk County district attorney sought to have the hearing moved to that county, and Justice Richard Goldberg denied the application. Suffolk County's appeal was dismissed by the Appellate Division. The hearing was held before Judge Goldberg at South Beach in the early spring of 1983. The director, represented by the attorney general, sought Ardito's conversion to civil status, which the district attorney opposed.

There was extensive testimony by the various psychiatrists, psychologists, and psychiatric social workers who had examined and treated Ardito during her six-year confinement, as well as by Zolan, who had again examined Ardito in 1980. The judge reviewed the reports of various experts and Ardito's hospital records from Mid-Hudson, Central Islip, and South Beach psychiatric centers. He also read the transcript of Ardito's 1980 examination by Zolan and listened to the tape recording of her 1980 examination by another independent psychiatrist, Dr. A. Louis McGarry. Ardito attended the hearing but did not testify.

On June 1, 1983, Judge Goldberg filed his decision. His ultimate conclusion was that Ardito had feigned mental illness over the years and had deliberately done so to avoid being placed on trial for the crimes charged. "Mrs. Ardito conveniently blocks out any inquiry into the persons and events surrounding her indictment and her memory lapses are both erratic and inconsistent with events both before and after the alleged crimes were committed," he wrote. "The type of amnesia she attempts to display has no known parallel in the annals of medical history."

Judge Goldberg supported this conclusion with a careful analysis of the overall record and proof presented at the hearing. The complete failure of the experts to agree on the same diagnosis indicated to him the absence of mental illness. He found that Ardito had intentionally faked her responses on various standard tests so as to appear less intelligent and more forgetful than she actually was and had deliberately misled the examiners. Her responses to Zolan showed her not to be stupid but instead quite capable of understanding the criminal charges and able to assist in her defense. In summary, Judge Goldberg concluded that Ardito was not incapacitated for purposes of retrial of the indictment. He denied conversion to civil status.

A FUGITIVE FROM JUSTICE

Ardito learned of Judge Goldberg's decision from another patient who had read about it, and she knew that the next step would be being brought to Riverhead for a retrial. On June 5, she walked off the unsecured grounds of South Beach Psychiatric Center and became a fugitive from justice. After the hospital staff noticed her absence, the Suffolk County district attorney was notified, and I signed a warrant for her arrest. The warrant and Ardito's photograph and description were immediately distributed to police agencies across the country.

During the summer and fall of 1983, there were four sightings of a woman believed to be Vikki Ardito in Vail, Colorado. The first was in early August in front of the Lodge at Vail by a Vail police officer. Several weeks later, a civilian police department employee saw the same woman in front of several local shops. In mid-October another local police officer saw the same woman at a shopping mall. Around the same time, another person saw the woman seated in the bar of a local restaurant. All four observers gave similar descriptions of age (forties), height (5' 7" to 5' 8"), weight (120–125 pounds) and hair ("brown with blonde streaks"), and when a Suffolk County detective visited Vail with Ardito's arrest photographs each said it was the same woman they had seen.

The woman observed in Vail and "positively identified" as Vikki Ardito was not her but rather a woman of strikingly similar appearance. Ardito had no funds when she fled South Beach and could not have traveled to Colorado and spent months in Vail, an expensive resort community. Ardito had an aunt who lived in Palmetto, Florida, and her mother often spent time there with the aunt. Palmetto was within the jurisdiction of the nearby Bradenton Police Department. In January 1984 that department began an investigation of contacts between Ardito and her mother. Through a confidential source they learned that Ardito was telephoning her mother in Palmetto from where she was living somewhere in the Tampa/St. Petersburg area and that her mother was sending her money using an intermediary. This information was provided to the Suffolk County district attorney, who dispatched detective George Latchford, the lead Mattana murder-case investigator, to Florida to work with the Bradenton police.

With the help of Latchford's knowledge of Ardito's history and habits, they were able to trace Ardito to an address in Tampa where she was living with Michelle Fisher, a close friend from New York, both using assumed names. Ardito was supporting herself by working as a housekeeper, laundress, and babysitter for several families in the Tampa area. On March 29, the Bradenton police learned that Ardito was visiting her mother in Palmetto and arrested her on the fugitive warrant. She waived extradition, and Latchford took her to Long Island by plane. Ardito was brought before me on April 3. She said she had no money to hire a lawyer, and I appointed attorney Eric Naiburg from the assigned murder counsel list. After I remanded her to jail without bail, she was examined by two psychiatrists, who both found she was not mentally incapacitated.

In June, attorney Michael Pollina of Mineola appeared as Ardito's attorney, and Naiburg was relieved. Ardito's ex-husband Gerald Ardito had hired Pollina to again represent her. He had previously hired Pollina to represent her in the original trial (Pollina had brought in John Sutter as trial counsel), and in several of the retention proceedings when Ardito was in South Beach.

SHIFTING STORIES

Pollina sought a conference with me, attended by Steven Wilutis, chief of the district attorney's trial bureau, who would be prosecuting Ardito on her retrial. He indicated that Ardito was prepared to plead guilty and sought a plea bargain with the district attorney. Wilutis said that under no circumstances would his office consent to a guilty plea to a lesser charge or recommend a minimum prison sentence of less than twenty-five years if Ardito were to plead guilty as charged. He refused to bargain with Ardito in any manner and offered no incentive for her to plead guilty.

At this June 26 conference, Pollina asked me to order a preplea investigation. In such an investigation, the defendant allows the probation department to examine the defendant's family background and situation, education, employment record and any criminal record, the recommendations of the prosecutor and others as to punishment and details of the offense charged and defendant's participation, and then report on all of it to the judge. The defendant is interviewed but not required to admit guilt. The department investigator and supervisor recommend a range of punishment should the defendant plead guilty.

During the following six weeks, a probation officer conducted an extensive investigation of Ardito's life history and the facts and circumstances of Benjamin Mattana's murder. Ardito was interviewed in depth, and she discussed her troubled marriage to Gerald Ardito and her separation to live with Mattana. The lead police investigators and the prosecutor were also interviewed and expressed their recommendations.

I also received many letters both in support and against leniency, some sent to the probation office and others mailed directly to me. The more than two dozen letters in support of Ardito praised her as a kind and generous person, a loving mother and someone who had a way with animals. The letters were from a wide spectrum of individuals who had known Ardito over her lifetime—family friends, business associates, even her dentist—and all thought her alleged criminal conduct inexplicable considering her many fine qualities.

The Roman Catholic priest/chaplain and the Society of Friends chaplain at the jail described Ardito's exemplary conduct as an inmate who befriended and helped other female inmates, and both recommended leniency. Several letter writers noted how traumatic the death of her nine-month-old son had been. As one said, "This, I think, was the turning point in her life." A lengthy letter from her lawyer claimed that Mattana had abused and threatened her. A letter from a parish priest who knew her decades earlier included a story that might appear damaging in light of her later crime: According to the priest, as a teenager Ardito arranged to have herself kidnapped and called her father from a pay phone to ask that he pay ransom.

I also received many letters asking that I impose the maximum sentence, including a moving one from Mattana's father, who spoke of his son's character, the toll his murder had taken on the family, and his bitterness toward Ardito. "Since the death of Benjie," he wrote, "my family has suffered immensely and have been torn apart." Describing himself as a recluse, he said visiting his son's grave once or twice a day was his main activity.

The probation officer and her supervisor both recommended that if Ardito pled guilty she be incarcerated as prescribed by law and that I determine an appropriate minimum period of imprisonment. Balancing the aggravating and mitigating factors in the case, I decided that should Ardito plead guilty as charged and fully admit the details of her criminal conduct, a fair and just sentence would be concurrent sentences of life imprisonment on the kidnapping and murder counts with a minimum period of eighteen years on each count.

I conferred with the attorneys on August 1, 1984, and informed them of my sentencing decision should Ardito plead guilty as charged. I let Pollina know that I would not bargain with Ardito on the proposed sentence, and he left to confer with her. Returning within an hour, he told me Ardito would not plead guilty and would rather go to trial. I fixed October 29, 1984, as the trial date, and the case was assigned to Judge Alfred Tisch of the County Court.

Pollina filed notice that Ardito intended to raise the defense of legal insanity and of having acted because of extreme emotional disturbance, and she was thereafter examined by psychiatrists in connection with these defenses. The district attorney prepared for Ardito's retrial by locating the witnesses who had testified against her in the 1977 trial and scheduling their appearance again. The district attorney also believed that Sebastian Ventimiglia and Mario Russo might be persuaded to testify against Ardito and had both brought to the local jail from their upstate prisons.

Ten days before the trial date, Ardito told Pollina that her ex-husband Gerald Ardito was involved in arranging for Mattana's murder and that she intended to disclose his culpability when she testified on her own behalf on the retrial. Pollina also learned that Ardito had described Gerald Ardito's involvement when she was examined by the psychiatrists in preparation for the insanity defense.

On October 29, the morning of the trial, Pollina told Judge Tisch about Ardito's statements and sought to be relieved of representing her. He claimed that because Gerald Ardito was compensating him, he had an attorney/client relationship with him as well as with Vikki Ardito and that it would be a conflict of interest for him to elicit the Gerald Ardito complicity testimony from Vikki during trial. Judge Tisch ruled that Pollina only represented Vikki Ardito, not her ex-husband, and denied relieving him of his responsibility. Pollina then asked Judge Tisch to delay the trial proceedings until later in the day to allow him and Steven Wilutis to confer with me about a possible disposition of the case by a guilty plea. Judge Tisch agreed.

Pollina and Wilutis came to my office later in the morning. Pollina told me that he intended to discuss with Ardito the possibility of her pleading guilty and wanted to be assured that my sentence proposal made on August 1 (three concurrent life sentences, each with eighteen-year minimums) was still available if Ardito pled guilty as charged to the entire indictment. I told him that it was available, but only for that day, because once the trial got underway any disposition would have to be before Judge Tisch, as I would then no longer be involved in the case.

It was now time for the luncheon recess, and Pollina asked to use my vacant courtroom during the recess to meet with Ardito and discuss the matter with her in comparative privacy. Pollina was confined to a wheelchair, and it was very difficult for him to move inside the holding cells to have a private conference with Ardito. I agreed, and the courtroom was locked during the recess. After the recess, Pollina told me that Ardito had decided to plead guilty, and arrangements were made to conduct the proceedings during the afternoon session.

SECOND THOUGHTS

Word quickly spread throughout the courthouse that Vikki Ardito was going to plead guilty, and the spectator section was nearly full when I entered the courtroom. Ardito was already seated at the counsel table closest to the bench. I'd permitted her to sit and speak during the proceeding, which was going to be somewhat lengthy for her to remain standing throughout. I questioned Ardito in detail as to her desire to plead guilty and thus waive her right to a trial and her right to raise defenses and give up her constitutional right to confront the witnesses against her. I asked her about her understanding of the charges contained in the indictment and the mandated sentences upon conviction. And I questioned her as to whether her decision to plead guilty was voluntary. I satisfied myself that she was doing this as a result of her own decision and that no person, including her attorney, was forcing her or applying pressure to make her plead guilty.

The court clerk then read each of the four counts of the indictment in their entirety, and Ardito pled guilty to each. The language included the details of the conspiracy, the kidnapping by having Mattana abducted from his Lloyd Harbor house, his being taken to Howard Beach and his murder by being shot to death at that location. In her own words, Ardito described how she hired Ventimiglia to kidnap and kill Mattana and stated that she fully intended to cause Mattana's death (a key legal element of intentional murder).

I directed that the preplea report be converted into a presentence report and brought up to date with a new interview of Ardito, now that she had admitted her guilt. I fixed December 11, 1984, as the sentencing date. Since a trial was not to take place, I signed an order directing the return of Ventimiglia and Russo to their upstate prisons. I often wondered whether they would have cooperated with the district attorney and testified against Ardito, which of course would have required each to admit under oath his own complicity in the crimes.

During the following weeks, Ardito was interviewed by a probation officer, and she was somewhat ambiguous in discussing her part in the kidnapping and murder, seeming to minimize her own conduct. She said she now believed that she should not have pled guilty but gave no reason for this belief. The first indication I had that she was having second thoughts was a handwritten letter I received from Ardito on November 28, stating that she was discharging Pollina as her attorney. She gave no reasons, and I was not to learn of her reason until a number of weeks later. Ardito was brought to court on December 11 and discharged Pollina on the record. The sentencing was adjourned for several weeks at Ardito's request to allow her to obtain new counsel. The Garden City law firm of Burns and Berger eventually entered the case as Ardito's attorneys. I do not know who was paying these new attorneys' fees. Pollina, whose fees had been paid by Gerald Ardito since 1976, was discharged by Vikki Ardito personally, and it is highly unlikely that her ex-husband was involved in retaining and paying different attorneys.

After several additional adjournments of the sentence date, Ardito's new attorneys brought a motion seeking permission for Ardito to withdraw her guilty pleas. In her papers, Ardito contended that she did not commit the crimes to which she pled guilty. She claimed that her former attorney Pollina was not acting on her behalf, but rather on her ex-husband's behalf, when she entered her guilty pleas, and lastly that she was induced to plead guilty by the district attorney's promise to obtain a favorable sentence for her daughter Deena in an unrelated drug case, a promise that was not fulfilled.

After reading Ardito's claims, the reason for her discharging Pollina was clear. As the date approached when she would be sentenced and transferred from her comparatively comfortable situation as one of the few female inmates in the local jail to the crowded upstate women's prison, Ardito considered possible ways to have her guilty pleas set aside. If one way was to put the blame on Pollina, she had to get him out of the picture before she could proceed with her effort.

The district attorney opposed Ardito's motion, and the matter was adjourned for several months to permit the parties to prepare for a hearing. The four-day hearing was held in late April 1985. Ardito testified that it was her ex-husband Gerald Ardito who had conspired with Ventimiglia and Russo to have Mattana kidnapped and murdered. She was only a forced bystander to the crimes. Gerald Ardito wanted her to be convicted of the crimes instead of him, she said, and Pollina was acting on his behalf in having her plead guilty. Ardito's attorneys had Ventimiglia brought from prison, and he tried to help Ardito by saying he was brought into the plan by Gerald Ardito.

I found Ardito's protestation of innocence totally unconvincing. From presiding over her original trial, I was familiar with all the evidence that incriminated her. Junior Dellacona's and James Pape's testimony was credible, and neither had a motive to falsely implicate Ardito in planning and carrying out the abduction and murder of Benjamin Mattana. Ardito's efforts to avoid a retrial by feigning mental illness and fleeing the jurisdiction when her acting was exposed by Judge Goldberg was not the conduct of an innocent person. When actually facing retrial, Ardito's intention to claim legal insanity or extreme emotional disturbance, which would permit a jury to excuse or reduce her criminal responsibility, was conduct hardly to be expected of a person claiming to be not guilty.

Her attempt to put her prior attorney Pollina in the position of knowing that Gerald Ardito was culpable and seeing her convicted in his place was especially incredible. According to Dellacona, Vikki Ardito told him that Gerald Ardito knew about her criminal plan and said to do it on her own. If that was true, Gerald Ardito may well have had some complicity in the events.

I was also satisfied after the hearing that there was no promise made by the district attorney to Ardito regarding her daughter's unrelated drug case. I found that Ardito's guilty pleas were voluntary in all respects. On June 3, 1985, I filed a written decision in which I determined that Ardito should not be permitted to withdraw her guilty pleas and directed her sentencing to take place.

A week later, Ardito wrote to me, asking that I reconsider my ruling and grant her "the full opportunity to prove to this court that I am not guilty of the crimes I've been accused." Referring to her past troubled emotional state, she said she entered the guilty plea in part because she did not know about information that would prove her innocence. Without mentioning her ex-husband by name, she again implied that he was behind the murder and attached two letters from Ventimiglia saying the same ("He instilled fear in me then. Well, I still fear, Vikki.") as well as urging her not to give up ("You've got this case BEAT!"). For her part, Ardito claimed that she wasn't capable of taking a human life. Regarding the Mattana murder, "My only involvement is being a compassionate human being."

THE CASE COMES TO AN END

Vikki Ardito was sentenced on June 20, 1985, just over nine years after the commission of her crimes. On the criminal conspiracy count I imposed a prison sentence of six to eighteen years; on the kidnapping count, a prison sentence of eighteen years to life; on the intentional murder count, a sentence of eighteen years to life; and on the felony murder count, a sentence of eighteen years to life. I directed that all four sentences be served concurrent with each other. On the following day, Ardito was taken to the women's prison at Bedford Hills in upper Westchester County and became state inmate number 8500297.

Three weeks after her arrival she continued her effort to reverse her convictions by appealing my decision denying her permission to withdraw her guilty pleas to the Appellate Division in Brooklyn. Claiming indigence, her appeal was assigned to Louise Perrotta, a staff attorney of the Suffolk County Legal Aid Society's appeal bureau. In December 1986, while her appeal was still pending and not yet submitted, Ardito sought executive clemency from Governor Cuomo. Having by then served the prerequisite half of her eighteen-year minimum sentence—the nine years calculated by combining six years of criminal status confinement in psychiatric hospitals and a total of three years confinement in local jail and state prison—she hoped to persuade the governor that early release was appropriate in her case.

My opinion was sought, and I stated several reasons why clemency should not be granted: Ardito was the instigator of the murder plan and hired the gunman; her six-year hospital confinement hardly compared to that in jail or prison, even though it was counted as the same; she was not admitting her guilt; and she was attempting to have her convictions reversed at the same time she was seeking clemency for her conduct. What's more, I wrote, "Her feigned illness and her escape clearly demonstrate her guilt in this matter." The district attorney and the murder victim's father also opposed Ardito's application, with Mattana Sr. noting that "Benjie was a very warm-hearted and loving son ... When Benjie died a part of me died with him." The governor did not act on the request.

It was only after Ardito's clemency request was concluded with no action that I learned that in the fall of 1985 Ardito was found to have cancer in her right lung and had been transferred to Westchester County Medical Center, where the lung was surgically removed. I do not know whether Ardito disclosed this as a reason to be granted clemency.

On May 4, 1987, Ardito's legal aid attorney brought a proceeding in the Supreme Court to have her convictions vacated because of alleged improper and prejudicial conduct in connection with Ardito's guilty pleas. Ardito claimed in her affidavit that my courtroom was locked and the public excluded while she was entering her guilty pleas. To support this allegation, she attached an affidavit of Michelle Fisher, her close friend and her companion in Tampa while she was a fugitive. Fisher claimed that she was in the courthouse at Riverhead on October 29, 1984, when Ardito's retrial was to begin and learned that Ardito intended to plead guilty in my courtroom. She said she hurried to my courtroom, intending to confront and stop Ardito from pleading guilty, and upon arrival found the doors locked. The court officers forcibly prevented her physical attempt to open the doors.

Because I was the person accused of judicial misconduct by allegedly ordering the public barred from an open courtroom, and would be testifying in the proceeding, the entire matter was assigned to another judge, Paul T. D'Amaro. The district attorney asked Judge D'Amaro for a reasonable time to investigate and answer the allegations. Ardito's attorney strongly objected, claiming that her client's poor health must be considered. She told the judge that Ardito's original cancer had spread to her kidney, and that organ had been surgically removed in late January 1987. The cancer then spread to her left lung, and the lower lobe was surgically removed in early March 1987. The surgeon was of the opinion that the cancer would continue to spread and that Ardito would probably be dead within six months. Ardito's attorney candidly admitted that in the bringing this proceeding, her hope was to obtain a speedy determination of the propriety of her convictions so as to enable Ardito to be released from prison before she died.

The district attorney and I filed affidavits setting forth the facts of what actually occurred in my courtroom on October 29, 1984. We explained that the vacant courtroom was closed to the public and locked during the luncheon recess to allow Ardito and her attorney to consult in private regarding a guilty plea, and that when the courtroom was opened to admit the public for the afternoon session many persons who had learned of Ardito's intention to plead guilty gathered to observe the proceedings. When Ardito was brought from the holding cell into the courtroom Fisher, who was seated in the first row of spectators, rose from her seat and attempted to approach Ardito, shouting loudly, "Vikki, don't do it!" Fisher continued to scream at Ardito, begging her not to plead guilty, and two court officers had to physically restrain her. She resisted them and had to be forcibly removed to the lobby.

All of this was occurring as I was about to enter the courtroom, and I overheard Fisher's shouting. Fisher attempted and was prevented from reentering the courtroom but continued her loud pleading through the now closed but unlocked doors. After the submission of all the documents in the proceeding, Judge D'Amaro heard oral argument from both attorneys on June 1, 1987. He reserved his decision, permitting both sides to submit legal memoranda.

By August 24, 1987, Ardito's condition had worsened. She was granted medical leave and admitted to Calvary Hospital in the Bronx, where she could more easily be visited by her children and sister. Frances Victoria Ardito, known to all as Vikki, died there on September 14, 1987, at age fifty-one. Judge D'Amaro dismissed the undecided proceeding as moot, and the pending appeal was also dismissed by the Appellate Division for the same reason. As the final legal step of the Benjamin Mattana murder prosecution, I dismissed the indictment on January 19, 1988, and the case became history.

EPILOGUE

Sebastian Ventimiglia was denied release on parole eight times since first becoming eligible and was ultimately released after his ninth parole board hearing on July 25, 2013. He had been imprisoned in local jails and various New York state prisons for nearly thirty-seven years. Now sixty-five years old, he completed college and graduate school while in prison, taught a course in theology, and served as an aide in a mental health unit. An avid exerciser, he attempted to get a book about his behind-bars fitness regimen published. He married Angela, a funeral director, before his release. Mario Russo was imprisoned in local jail and various New York state prisons for nearly twenty-four years and was released on parole on November 3, 2000. He was immediately turned over to the United States immigration authorities as an undocumented alien.

The Benjamin Mattana murder and the subsequent twelve-year saga of his murderer Vikki Ardito are little remembered by Long Islanders and others today, except by those who had a role in the investigation and prosecution or in Ardito's post-mistrial medical and legal proceedings. But in 1993 a remarkable reprise of the Ardito/Mattana murder case took place in Manhattan, and it involved Gerald (Jed) Ardito, Ardito's older son, who at age seventeen in 1976 had been taught the martial arts by Ventimiglia.

In his late twenties Ardito owned a temporary employment agency in Manhattan, and in 1988 he hired nineteen-year-old Marie Daniele as a sales representative. They became romantically involved the following year and were engaged to be married. However, the relationship ended in late 1990 when Ardito became involved with another woman. Daniele went to work with another temporary employment agency, where she eventually attained executive rank. She resumed dating Ardito after he had married and then divorced the other woman. Daniele subsequently broke off the relationship but kept in touch with Ardito.

At 2:50 a.m. on February 18, 1993, Daniele, who had been visiting Ardito at his apartment on West Forty-Ninth Street, was heard screaming for help and was seen by neighbors on the staircase outside the apartment with Ardito's hands on her throat. One neighbor got a baseball bat and forced Ardito to release Daniele while another called 911. Daniele refused to press charges and told Ardito she did not want to see him again. Two months later, on the morning of April 28, 1993, Ardito registered at the Grand Hyatt Hotel on Forty-Second Street. Perhaps hoping for a reconciliation, Ardito invited Daniele to join him for lunch and purchased jewelry to give her. She agreed and came to his hotel room number 3431, where he ordered room service lunch for two.

Later that afternoon, Ardito contacted attorney James LaRossa and

     THOMAS M. STARK

told him that Daniele was in the hotel room, apparently dead after they had had sexual relations. (LaRossa had represented Vikki Ardito in her first retention hearing in 1978.) The lawyer called the Manhattan district attorney's office. The police went to the hotel and upon entering the room found Daniele's partially undressed body on the floor. Death had been caused by manual strangulation. The next day Ardito was arrested and charged with Daniele's murder. The authorities told the *New York Times* that the theme of a broken romance, an attempted reconciliation, and then a murder was an apparent reprise of the events involving Ardito's mother, Frances Victoria Ardito, in 1976. (This was not quite accurate. Vikki Ardito was not attempting a reconciliation with Mattana; rather, she was attempting to rid herself of him.)

Ardito went on trial in November 1994 and was convicted of manslaughter by the jury. He attempted a "rough sex" defense on trial, claiming that Daniele died accidentally during erotic asphyxia to enhance sexual pleasure. The jury rejected this defense but convicted Ardito of a less serious degree of homicide. Ardito was sentenced to a prison term of eight and one-third to twenty-five years, and his conviction was affirmed on appeal. He was released on parole on December 23, 2009, after serving fourteen years in the New York state prison system.

The family of Frances Victoria Ardito is unique in the annals of crime. With a mother who at age thirty-nine has her unfaithful paramour murdered and dies at age fifty-one during her imprisonment for her crime, a daughter who at age twenty-seven went to jail for the sale of illegal drugs and a son who at age thirty-four was arrested for the strangulation killing of his ex-fiancé, there may not be another family group to match it.

PART 3

The Irate Deli Proprietor
The Josefsek Family Murders
May 10, 1980

Anthony Cisco, arrested on May 13, 1980,
for the murders of a mother and three children

A DEADLY FEUD

In the spring of 1980, John Josefsek and his family—including his thirty-one-year-old wife Maureen and his three children, eleven-year-old John Michael, nine-year-old Colleen, and four-year-old Cathleen—resided in a modest ranch house at 11 Norton Drive in East Northport, Long Island. Norton Drive runs easterly from its beginning at Vernon Valley Road, a main north/south highway leading to the East Northport railroad station, which is located half a mile south of the Norton Drive intersection. The Josefsek house was several hundred yards east of Vernon Valley Road, at the top of a rise in the roadway.

The Roadside Delicatessen was on the west side of Vernon Valley Road, immediately north of the Genola Rural Cemetery and directly opposite Norton Drive. The proprietor of the delicatessen was Anthony Cisco, a thirty-eight-year-old navy veteran. His wife, Patricia, helped in the store, which was generally known as Tony's Deli. The Ciscos employed a nineteen-year-old local boy, Andrew Hahn, as a part-time clerk on weekends.

The deli was somewhat of a hangout for local youths, who congregated in its parking lot or drank beer in nearby woods, leaving empty cans and bottles behind. There were suspicions among the neighbors that young people were able to purchase beer there without proof of legal age and that illegal drugs were also being sold. The Suffolk County police were aware of these suspicions but had no proof to support arrests. Police cars occasionally visited the deli to break up groups of young people who had become unruly. One neighbor later told the *New York Times*, "We are all so sick of this problem. We've called the police so many times. They come and chase them away and then they are back the next night."

The deli was clearly visible from the nearby Josefsek house, and vice versa. John Josefsek had seen youths leaving the deli with what appeared to be cans of beer and drinking them in a wooded area near his house. He went to the deli, introduced himself as a neighbor who lived up Norton Drive and asked Anthony Cisco if he was checking proof of legal age before selling beers to minors. Cisco told him that he believed the beer was being purchased legally and given to minors outside the store.

After his visit, Cisco began to believe that Josefsek was watching the deli from his house and calling the police when he observed youths patronizing the store and drinking beer outside. Cisco became obsessed with this belief and claimed that the police visits were discouraging young people from coming to the deli, hurting his business. On April 12, 1980, Frank Bucaria, another East Northport delicatessen owner, came to Cisco's store, where they discussed the problem of minors purchasing and drinking beer outside the deli. Cisco pointed up Norton Drive to the Josefsek house, saying, "That guy up there is busting balls and calling the cops about the kids."

Matthew Oresky of East Northport was a steady customer of Tony's Deli and knew Cisco well. On May 5, 1980, a friend, Bill Foley, gave Oresky a surplus US Army M-18 smoke grenade, and he and some friends detonated the grenade in a vacant outdoor lot to see how it worked and what it did. The grenade was housed in a storage canister and had to be removed before use. It was armed by removing a pin, and a safety handle had to be released before the grenade could be detonated. After the handle was released, there was a delay of several seconds before the device exploded, emitting a long flame from the base and a large amount of colored and acrid smoke.

Oresky wanted more smoke grenades, and on May 7 purchased two of the same type and model at GI George's, a local military supply store. Stephen Parkinson, the store's proprietor, warned Oresky that the grenade's explosion produced extreme heat and that the smoke could suffocate a person if detonation occurred in an enclosed indoor area. The device was intended to be used outdoors.

That same afternoon Oresky went to Cisco's deli to repay money

     THOMAS M. STARK

he owed and brought one of the smoke grenades with him. Cisco was interested in the grenade and asked how it worked. Oresky showed him how to detonate the grenade and explained that it got very hot when it exploded and produced a lot of smoke. He gave the grenade to Cisco in payment of the money he owed the deli. Before Oresky left, Cisco mentioned the man "up the hill," who he said was complaining about beer sales to minors and calling the police. If the man came to the store again, Cisco said, he intended to punch him.

The store clerk Hahn stopped by the deli on the evening of May 8, and Cisco showed him the smoke grenade. Saying he wanted to get more grenades to sell in the deli, he asked Hahn to find out where to get them. On the following day, May 9, a Friday, Hahn and his friend Cliff Leary asked several others if they knew where to obtain smoke grenades, explaining that Tony Cisco wanted them. Leary dropped Hahn at the deli that evening for work and invited him to come to a party later that night at his house. His parents were away, and he was having friends over. Hahn said he would come after finishing work.

Three Suffolk County police cars came to the deli at 7:30 p.m., and the youths who had gathered in the deli parking lot scattered. One officer told Cisco they had received an anonymous call complaining about youths drinking beer and causing a disturbance outside the deli. Jeffrey Hamilton, a regular customer, came by the deli while the police were there and parked his car out front. While he was inside an officer placed a ticket on his car for an obstructed windshield (several items hanging from the rear-view mirror). After Hamilton came out and found the ticket, he went back inside and told Cisco. Cisco said the cops were there because the man up the hill, Josefsek, had called them and that he was "going to get even with him."

After Hamilton left, Cisco told Hahn that business was bad right now, that there were no kids around because Josefsek had called the cops, and that he wanted to "get the message to him and get even." Hahn suggested putting the Josefsek garden hose into a basement window and flooding it. Cisco said he had a better idea. Taking Hahn into the rear of the store, Cisco took out the smoke grenade and said Hahn could throw it into the Josefsek house. Hahn agreed to do it, and he and Cisco planned to go to the Josefsek house later that night, where Hahn would throw the grenade.

"OH MY GOD. I KILLED SOMEONE."

Few customers came into the deli during the next hour and a half until Bobby DiCarlo, another regular, showed up at about 9:30 p.m. Cisco, Hahn, and DiCarlo got into a discussion about the cops coming by earlier that night and scaring off customers. Cisco told DiCarlo of the plan to throw the smoke grenade into the Josefsek house, and the three discussed the details. Because his van might be recognized, Cisco said they shouldn't use it and told Hahn to get someone to drive him. At 10:30 p.m. Hahn called a friend, nineteen-year-old Andrew Letkovsky (who also went by Andreas), and asked him to drive to the deli to pick him up. Letkovsky soon arrived, and Cisco, Hahn, and Letkovsky went into the rear room, where DiCarlo had remained. Cisco took out the grenade from its container, and he and Hahn told Letkovsky of the plan to throw the grenade into the Josefsek house and why they were doing it.

Cisco showed Hahn and Letkovsky how to arm the grenade and release the handle before throwing it. He suggested that Hahn throw the grenade through a basement window, but DiCarlo thought an upstairs window would be better. Agreeing, Cisco told Hahn to throw it through the large bow window in the front of the house. It would burn a hole in the rug, Cisco maintained, and the smoke would dirty up the house. He told Hahn to wait until the Josefsek family had gone to bed and to wear a heavy shirt to avoid getting burned. Hahn said he and Letkovsky were first going to the party at Cliff Leary's house and would leave there later to go to the Josefsek house to throw the grenade.

At 10:45 p.m., Hahn and Letkovsky left the deli and drove to Leary's house in Northport. Upon arriving, Hahn called Leary out to the car, showed him the grenade and told him of the plan to throw it into the Josefsek house, adding that Cisco was the instigator of the plan. Hahn and Letkovsky then joined the other youths at the party going on in the house. A while later, Hahn went out to the car and brought the grenade into the house, where he showed it to the others. He said it was a fragmentation grenade, which he planned to explode later on a vacant lot.

Shortly after midnight, Hahn invited Leary to go with him and Letkovsky on the trip to the Josefsek house, and he asked Leary about protective clothing to wear when he threw the grenade. Leary provided him with a jacket, gloves, hat, and goggles. The three left Leary's house at 12:30 a.m. and drove to the Josefsek house. Noticing that there was still a light on inside, they drove around for fifteen minutes before returning and finding the house darkened. (Colleen and Cathleen Josefsek had gone to bed at 9:00 p.m. the previous evening, John Michael Josefsek and Maureen Josefsek at 10:00 p.m., and John Josefsek at 10:45 p.m. Before retiring, John Josefsek had left a light on in the living room with a timer set to turn it off after midnight.)

Letkovsky parked with the headlights out, and Hahn put on the jacket, gloves, hat, and goggles. He walked across the front lawn and stopped five feet in front of the bow window. Pulling the arming pin and releasing the handle, he threw the grenade through the glass and ran back to the car. As he was getting in, Letkovsky and Leary saw a flash inside the broken bow window. They drove away quickly and returned to Leary's house.

The smoke grenade landed and detonated on a living room sofa situated immediately under the shattered bow window. A copious amount of acrid, greenish-colored smoke was generated and quickly spread throughout the living room and the hallway and into the three bedrooms where the Josefsek family members were sleeping. As it detonated, the grenade emitted a column of flame from its base, igniting the couch, which with its foam rubber cushion began to burn quickly and in turn ignited the ceiling above.

A man named Heinz Schlueter passed the Josefsek home on his way home and saw the interior fire through the shattered bow window. He stopped at the house but was unable to enter any of the doors to awaken the sleeping occupants. Police officer Douglas Darrell was on sector car patrol on Vernon Valley Road, and as he passed Norton Drive at 12:54 a.m., he saw the fire burning in the Josefsek house. He drove up Norton Drive to the house while reporting the fire by radio. He first went to the front door, where the heat was too intense to attempt entry, and then went around the house seeking other entrances.

John Josefsek, awakened by the smoke and heat filling the master bedroom, rolled out of bed, opened a bedroom window and was able to climb through it to the ground outside. There he encountered Officer Darrell and told him his wife and children were still inside. Josefsek was practically insane trying to get back into the house. As he and Darrell attempted unsuccessfully to enter through other windows, they saw that the entire living room and hallway were now ablaze. Darrell pulled the patrol car under the daughters' bedroom window, where Josefsek, standing on the car hood, broke the window and was able to pull four-year-old Cathleen out.

Kenneth Hahn (not related to Andrew Hahn), assistant chief of the East Northport volunteer fire department, was alerted to the fire and its location by telephone at 12:58 a.m. and responded directly to the burning house. Arriving within minutes, he appraised the situation and radioed for further assistance. Finding the soot-covered child Cathleen Josefsek lying on front lawn not breathing, Hahn attempted resuscitation and radioed for ambulances to respond.

Other firefighters arrived, and three wearing Scott air packs entered the house through bedroom windows and removed Maureen, John Michael, and Colleen Josefsek, all of whom were soot-covered, hot, and not breathing. Firemen attempted to resuscitate all three. Ambulances arrived shortly, and the four victims were taken first to Huntington

Hospital, then without delay to Cornell Medical Center in New York City. (Cathleen Josefsek died en route to the city, and the three other victims died later that day and early the following day at Cornell Medical Center.) After the victims were removed from the burning house, the firemen extinguished the fire, using fog nozzles so as to not disturb the unburned furnishings.

When Andrew Hahn returned to the Leary house, he told the partygoers to listen for the sound of fire engines—they should be hearing them any minute, because he had thrown the grenade into a house on Norton Drive and started a fire. Hahn and Letkovsky returned to the fire, saw the ambulances and a stretcher at the scene, and quickly returned to the Leary house, where Hahn, distressed and crying, exclaimed to those present, "Oh my God, I killed someone. All I did was throw the grenade through the living room window." He said he had gotten the grenade from "Tony at the deli," who had told him where to throw it.

A CONSPIRACY UNCOVERED

When the fire was completely extinguished, Chief Hahn entered the house to investigate the origin and cause of the fire. Upon his arrival he had noticed that the smoke in the house was an unusual color—a dark grayish silver, which was not normal for a house fire. From the pattern and direction of the flames on the living room and hallway walls, he was able to place the origin of the fire at the completely consumed foam rubber living room couch. He noticed that the ceiling above the couch was burned open to the rafters in the attic and the roof holed above the area.

Because of the suspicious nature of the fire, the Suffolk County Police Department arson squad was notified, and Detective Dodd Amrhein of that squad came to the scene at 2:00 a.m. Chief Hahn told Amrhein of the unusual color of the smoke he had noticed and pointed out what he had observed after entering the burned house. Amrhein carefully examined both the exterior and interior of the house, noting the extent and type of smoke and fire damage throughout. He found no electrical malfunction or inflammable liquids that could have caused the fire. Lying on the bare springs of the burned couch, Amrhein and Hahn noticed a metal cylinder six inches long and two and one-half inches in diameter, which had been subjected to exterior and interior burns. Amrhein recognized it as probably part of an incendiary device that had ignited on the couch itself, starting the fire there and emitting the colored smoke that Hahn had seen. Amrhein accordingly reported to his squad commander his opinion that the fire was an act of arson.

After the first victim died and the fire had been deemed an arson, the police department homicide squad was notified. At 5:30 a.m., it took over the investigation. At 8:00 a.m., Andrew Hahn, still distressed over what he had seen at the scene when he returned there with Letkovsky while the firefighting was in progress, called Cisco, who told him that a little girl had died in the fire and that he should come to the deli.

Hahn walked to the deli, arriving in early afternoon. Telling Hahn that another person had died, Cisco asked him who else knew what he and Letkovsky had done. Hahn mentioned Cliff Leary. Cisco told Hahn to get in touch with Leary and Letkovsky and have them come to the deli as soon as possible. Leary arrived at the deli at 2:00 p.m., and Cisco told him and Hahn to say nothing to anybody; Hahn said Leary could be trusted. Cisco said he wished none of this had happened, but as it had, they both were to "stay cool." Letkovsky arrived at the deli about 6:00 p.m. and said he was shocked at what had happened. Told by Cisco to say nothing and "stay cool," Letkovsky observed that Cisco himself seemed "cool" about everything.

On Sunday, May 11, Hahn went to the deli in the early afternoon. The third victim had died the night before, and Cisco had learned the police were now investigating. He asked Hahn what had happened to the grenade's arming pin and release handle before he threw it through the window, and Hahn said he didn't know but assumed they were both in the Josefsek front yard where they fell.

     THOMAS M. STARK

Throughout the weekend the local media and radio stations continued their reports on the fire at the Josefsek house, including the fact that the police believed it was arson and that a sleeping mother and her three young children had tragically died. Donna Jones, a seventeen-year-old East Northport high school student, had attended the party at the Leary house on the night of May 9. She had seen the smoke grenade that Hahn had brought to the party, and Jones was present when Hahn returned to the party after leaving for a short while with Letkovsky and Leary and said he had thrown the grenade into a house on Norton Drive and started a fire. Jones also heard Hahn say he had gotten the grenade from Tony Cisco at the deli, and that Cisco had told him where to throw it. Knowing who started the fire and how he did it, she became distressed as she learned of the family deaths.

When Jones went to school on Monday, May 12, she decided she must tell someone in authority what she knew and settled on her high school guidance counselor. After hearing Jones's story, the guidance counselor insisted that she tell the police and brought her to the Second Precinct headquarters in nearby Huntington (also calling Jones's mother). Jones told detectives of Hahn, Letkovsky, and Leary leaving the house party for a short while and Hahn's statements upon their return. She described the grenade in great detail—the green color, dimensions she likened to a can of Coke, and that it had an attached ring and a handle—and even drew a sketch of it. Jones told the detectives where Hahn said he had gotten the grenade, what Tony Cisco had directed him to do with it, and his reaction after learning people had been hurt, how he kept screaming, "Oh my God," over and over again.

The second squad detectives who had taken Jones's oral statement notified the homicide squad, which sent two of its own detectives to Huntington and brought Jones and her mother to homicide squad headquarters in Hauppauge. Once there, Jones repeated what she had told the Second Squad detectives, and her oral statement was put in writing, which she signed at 6:45 p.m. Earlier that afternoon, after Jones had given the police a detailed description of the grenade, officers had gone to the Josefsek house and searched the lawn in the vicinity of the broken living room bow window. Embedded in the grass were the grenade's arming pin with ring and the release handle.

Jones had also told the police that she had been accompanied to the Leary house party by Douglas Lamb of East Northport. At 5:00 p.m., homicide squad detectives went to Lamb's home, and he agreed to go with them to Hauppauge headquarters, where he was interrogated as to what he knew of the events both preceding and after the Josefsek house fire. What he told the detectives was similar to Jones's story, from Hahn showing the smoke grenade to the partygoers and telling them of getting it from Cisco to what he said to the group when he returned about having thrown the grenade into a house on Norton Drive and how they should listen for fire sirens. Lamb's oral statement was incorporated into a lengthy written one, which he signed at 8:00 p.m.

Based upon the information provided by Jones and Lamb, homicide squad detectives Dennis Rafferty and Edward Halverson were directed to pick up Hahn and Leary for questioning. Earlier in the evening, the two men, learning that the police were looking for them, had contacted Letkovsky, who drove all three of them to the deli. Cisco told them that if the police were to question any of them, they should say they had never left the party at the Leary house.

Not finding Leary at his home, Rafferty was advised by police radio that Leary and Hahn were coming into the area by bicycle, and the detectives parked nearby. At 7:00 p.m., Rafferty stopped Leary and Hahn and ordered both to get into the police vehicle. They were driven to squad headquarters in Hauppauge, where they were placed in separate offices for interrogation, Leary by Halverson and Hahn by Rafferty.

Rafferty, with Detective James Cassidy present, told Hahn that they wanted to speak with him about the fatal fire the previous Friday night in East Northport and advised him of his Miranda rights. Hahn said he understood his rights, did not want to contact a lawyer and was willing to talk without a lawyer present. Rafferty questioned Hahn as to his involvement with the fire, and Hahn stated that he was at the Leary house party at the time of the fire and had nothing to do with it.

Detective Halverson called Rafferty out of the room and told him

     THOMAS M. STARK

that Leary had implicated Hahn in the throwing of the smoke grenade into the Josefsek house while he and Letkovsky waited in a car parked nearby. Returning to the interrogation room, Rafferty told Hahn what Leary had said and urged him to tell them his version of the events. Holding his head in his hands, Hahn responded, "I can't believe this happened. I didn't want the people to die." Hahn added that he couldn't live with this thing, that it had been bothering him since the fire, and he'd had trouble eating.

Rafferty asked Hahn to tell them what had happened, and Hahn made a lengthy oral incriminatory statement as to his participation in the crimes. Hahn agreed to sign a written statement containing all that he had admitted, and after this was prepared, Hahn signed it at 9:45 p.m. Hahn was then shown a police manual containing descriptions and drawings of various incendiary and explosive devices, in particular a US military smoke bomb. That device, Hahn said, was similar to the one he was given by Anthony Cisco—and the one he had thrown through the window of the Josefsek house.

THE TRIO ARRESTED

Based upon the information contained in Hahn, Leary, Jones, and Lamb's statements—and with Hahn's statement specifically implicating Anthony Cisco in the crimes under investigation—homicide squad detectives Thomas Schmitt and William Donohue were directed to proceed to The Roadside Deli in East Northport and arrest Cisco. Both officers arrived at the deli about 9:45 p.m. and encountered a man working in the front of the store. After Donohue identified himself as a police detective, the man acknowledged he was Anthony Cisco. Donohue told Cisco he was under arrest for arson, handcuffed him, and placed him in the police car. Patricia Cisco ran out of the deli to the police car screaming hysterically. Cisco told his wife not to worry, that he would call her, and he gave the deli keys to Schmitt to give to Patricia. She quickly grabbed the keys and went back into the deli.

Shortly after the trip back to Hauppauge started, Schmitt advised Cisco of his Miranda rights. Cisco said he understood his rights, did not want to contact a lawyer and was willing to talk to them without a lawyer. Asked whether he was involved with the Josefsek house fire, Cisco denied any knowledge of the fire, stating that he only knew what he had read in the newspapers and heard around the neighborhood. Asked whether he knew any members of the Josefsek family, Cisco said he knew them only casually and had no problems with them. During the balance of the trip to Hauppauge, Cisco was not interrogated any further as to the crimes under investigation.

Upon arrival at Hauppauge at about 10:00 p.m., Cisco was taken to an office. Schmitt told Rafferty that Cisco was under arrest and that he had been advised of his Miranda rights in the police car, and he apprised him of the limited scope of his interrogation. Rafferty and Halverson then entered the office where Cisco was seated, and Rafferty introduced himself and his fellow detective. When asked, Cisco said he had already been advised of his Miranda rights in the police car. Rafferty began to interrogate Cisco as to his involvement in the crimes. Cisco denied any involvement, and Rafferty began to press him on this issue, eliciting further denials from Cisco. Rafferty then told Cisco that Andrew Hahn had already implicated him in the crimes.

At this point in the interrogation, Cisco broke down, saying he and his family were ruined, that he never expected anyone would die or get hurt in the fire. He believed John Josefsek was watching the deli from the front window of his house and calling the police whenever he saw youths congregating outside the deli drinking beer. Josefsek was also reporting that the deli owner was selling beer to underaged youths, Cisco said. When the police would come and break up the youths, that hurt his business. Cisco admitted acquiring the smoke grenade from a customer in early May and knowing that it would get very hot and could start a fire when detonated. He also said that he became very annoyed

     THOMAS M. STARK

at Josefsek and wanted to start a fire in his house that would burn the rugs and dirty up the house with smoke.

Under questioning, Cisco admitted that he showed Hahn how to arm the grenade and told him to throw it through the window of the Josefsek house the night of May 9–10. He described Hahn calling his friend Andrew Letkovsky to drive him to the Josefsek house. After the fire started, he told the police, he came to the deli and walked up the hill to watch the house burning. Rafferty asked Cisco if he would give the police a written statement containing his oral admissions, and Cisco agreed to do so.

In the meanwhile, Schmitt and Donohue returned to the deli and requested that Patricia Cisco accompany them to squad headquarters. When they arrived, they found her talking on the telephone. She told them a lawyer wished to speak with them. Schmitt took the phone and a man identifying himself as Mark Slavin, a lawyer from the Siben & Siben office, said that he was now representing Mr. and Mrs. Cisco and requested that the police no longer interrogate his clients.

Schmitt and Donohue left immediately and called the squad headquarters, advising them of the phone conversation and Slavin's request. In the meanwhile, Slavin telephoned homicide squad headquarters, and his call was put through to Rafferty, who was with Cisco, preparing to take his written statement. Slavin told Rafferty not to interrogate Cisco any further, and Rafferty handed the telephone to Cisco. From this point, 11:05 p.m., no police officer continued any interrogation of either Anthony or Patricia Cisco.

Meanwhile, Hahn told the detectives that he did not want to make any telephone calls and asked that he not be held overnight in the same holding cells as Cisco. The police agreed with this request, and Hahn was taken to the second precinct holding cells in Huntington, where he was lodged in detention, while Cisco was lodged in detention in the fourth precinct in Hauppauge, adjoining the homicide squad headquarters.

On the following day, Letkovsky was picked up by homicide squad detectives and taken to squad headquarters. After being advised of his Miranda rights, he said that he did not want to contact a lawyer and consented to an interrogation without one. Told that he had been implicated by Hahn and Cisco as the driver of the car used in the commission of the arson, Letkovsky admitted his complicity and agreed to sign a written statement.

The homicide squad advised the district attorney of the arrests of Cisco, Hahn, and Letkovsky and the incriminatory statements made by each. The district attorney determined that its office had sufficient evidence to present the case to a grand jury and seek an indictment against all three defendants.

FROM ACCOMPLICES TO WITNESSES

At the first session of the grand jury on May 15, seven witnesses appeared: Detective Dodd Amrhein of the arson squad, a witness who testified about Hahn seeking another grenade, and partygoers Donna Jones, Douglas Lamb, Cynthia Tulke, Warren Hahn (Andrew's brother), and Cliff Leary. (Leary had been granted immunity from prosecution.)

Six photographs of the fire damage to the Josefsek house and four reports of the autopsies performed by the medical examiner on the bodies of the fire victims were put in evidence. During the second session on May 16, Sergeant Bernard Davis, a US Army bomb technician, testified about the cylinder found on the couch springs and the arming pin and handle found on the Josefsek lawn, which he identified as components of a M-18 smoke grenade. He explained how this grenade operates and what happens when detonated, including the heat produced, flames emitted, the characteristics of the smoke, and the danger to humans if detonated inside a house.

Detective Dennis Rafferty of the homicide squad testified as to the interrogation of Hahn and Cisco on May 12 and the oral incriminatory statements made by each. The components of the detonated M-18 smoke grenade and the written incriminatory statements of Hahn and Letkovsky were put in evidence. The grand jury deliberated for several days and on May 19 filed an indictment accusing Anthony Cisco, Andrew Hahn, and Andrew Letkovsky of the crimes of conspiracy in the fourth degree, arson in the third degree, and murder in the second degree.

The types of murders the defendants were accused of were not *intentional* murders, that is they were not accused of intending the deaths of Maureen Josefsek, John Michael Josefsek, Colleen Josefsek, and Cathleen Josefsek when the arson was committed. The only intentional conduct they were accused of was damaging the Josefsek house by starting a fire, that is, the felony of arson in the third degree. The first type of murder they were accused of was what is known as felony murder, in this case committing murder by committing arson and, in course of and in furtherance of such crime, causing the deaths of a victim by starting a fire, inflicting injuries that caused the victim's death.

The second type of murder they were accused of was what is known as depraved indifference reckless murder, in this case committing murder by recklessly engaging in conduct that created a grave risk of death to a victim, under circumstances evincing a depraved indifference to human life, by starting a fire that inflicted injuries that caused the victim's death. The eight counts of murder contained in the indictment included two for each victim, one for felony murder and one for depraved indifference reckless murder. The indictment was assigned to Judge Robert W. Doyle.

Both Hahn and Letkovsky were represented by retained counsel, and after their arraignment they were remanded to the custody of the sheriff and held at the Suffolk County jail without bail. Cisco told the judge he had no funds to hire counsel, and accordingly Judge Doyle assigned counsel, attorney William O'Leary, selected from the murder list maintained by the administrator of the assigned counsel plan. Cisco was also remanded without bail.

Letkovsky and Cisco, scheduled to go to court the same day for arraignment on the indictments, were being held in the same holding cell at the jail, awaiting transportation to the courthouse. Cisco told Letkovsky that Hahn "had really fucked out on us" and that he had spoken to some people upstate about getting rid of Hahn. Saying "we should dump the whole thing on Hahn," Cisco tried to convince Letkovsky to go along with this. Letkovsky told Cisco that he had not "ratted him out" to the police. This was a falsehood. Letkovsky had told the homicide detectives the whole story, which implicated Cisco in the arson of the Josefsek house.

The prosecution of Cisco, Hahn, and Letkovsky was assigned to assistant district attorney Thomas J. Spota. During the summer, Maurice Nadjari, Letkovsky's attorney, discussed with Spota his client's willingness to testify against Cisco and Hahn and his willingness to plead guilty to a reduced charge in satisfaction of the entire indictment. Spota agreed with Nadjari's offer and thereafter conducted extensive interviews of Letkovsky, who had been released from custody upon posting bail.

On September 18 Nadjari, Spota, and Letkovsky appeared before Judge Doyle. Nadjari advised the judge that his client wished to withdraw his plea of not guilty and plead guilty to attempted arson in the third degree. Spota advised the judge of Letkovsky's cooperation with the district attorney's office in preparing for trial and his agreement to testify for the prosecution on trial. Noting that Letkovsky, a college student with only minor traffic violations on his record, was essentially just the driver, Spota added that he was least culpable of the three defendants. Spota said he had made no agreement for any specific sentence recommendation to induce the guilty plea. For all these reasons, the district attorney was consenting to the plea in satisfaction of the entire indictment.

Judge Doyle questioned Letkovsky as to his understanding of what he was doing and permitted the guilty plea. Letkovsky then entered his guilty plea and acknowledged the truth of the contents of his May 13 incriminatory written statement. No sentencing date was fixed until after the Cisco/Hahn trial.

Due to the number of trials already scheduled on Judge Doyle's calendar, the Cisco/Hahn trial was transferred by the administrative judge to the Criminal Term of the Supreme Court, where I was presiding and had an open calendar. Cisco and Hahn had moved to suppress their incriminatory statements made on May 12: Cisco's oral statement before Detectives Rafferty and Halverson and Hahn's oral and written statements before Detectives Rafferty and Cassidy. I conducted an evidentiary hearing on the motion on October 20, 21, and 24 and found that their statements were not obtained in violation of their rights under the Fifth and Sixth Amendments to the US Constitution.

On November 3, the day that the trial was scheduled to begin, Andrew Hahn's attorney advised me that Hahn wished to withdraw his not guilty plea and to plead guilty to manslaughter in the first degree in satisfaction of the entire indictment. Spota advised me that Hahn had agreed to testify for the prosecution in Cisco's trial, and that the district attorney had made no agreement to recommend any particular sentence to induce Hahn's guilty plea. The district attorney's office was consenting to the plea in satisfaction of the entire indictment.

I questioned Hahn extensively as to his knowledge of what he was doing and satisfied myself that he was entering the guilty plea voluntarily, and accordingly permitted the plea. Hahn then pled guilty to manslaughter in the first degree and acknowledged the truthfulness of the contents of his May 12 written incriminatory statement. I deferred fixing a sentencing date until after the conclusion of the Cisco trial.

UNCONVINCING DENIALS

After Hahn's guilty plea, we proceeded to selection of a jury in the Cisco trial. After three days, a jury of eleven men and one woman was chosen, along with three male alternates. After opening statements by Spota and O'Leary, the prosecution presented its proof over a period of seven days with the testimony of twenty-six witnesses and the receipt into evidence of fourteen exhibits, including photographs of the fire-damaged home and what remained of the grenade.

Eleven police officers testified. These included the homicide squad detectives who interrogated Cisco, Hahn, and Letkovsky and took their incriminating statements. Chief Kenneth Hahn of the East Northport Fire Department testified, as well as the men who acquired and provided the smoke grenade to Cisco. Kenneth Snow, a forensic chemist with the US Treasury Department, identified the cylinder found on the Josefsek couch bedsprings and the arming pin and the handle found in the yard as being parts from a M-18 smoke grenade.

Darold Kelly, an ammunition specialist with the US Department of Defense, exhibited to the jury a live M-18 smoke grenade and explained how it worked and the dangerous conditions created by its detonation. Dr. John Grauerholz, the Suffolk County deputy medical examiner who performed the autopsies upon Maureen Josefsek and her three children, testified that each had died of burns to the body and smoke and carbon dioxide inhalation. John Josefsek, Donna Jones, and Cliff Leary also testified.

The two most important witnesses for the district attorney were Andrew Hahn and Andrew Letkovsky. Hahn testified about Cisco's remarks concerning his belief that John Josefsek was calling the police each time he saw youths drinking beer outside the deli, leading the police to come and the youths to disperse. Because of this, Hahn told the jury, Cisco said he had to get even with Josefsek.

Hahn described Cisco giving him the smoke grenade, showing him how to arm it and throw it after releasing the handle, and directing him to throw the grenade through the front bow window of the Josefsek house after all the occupants were asleep. The resulting fire, Cisco said, would burn just the rug, and the smoke would only dirty up the house. Hahn's testimony also covered going to the Josefsek house after midnight with Letkovsky driving and Leary along as a passenger, walking from the car, and arming and throwing the grenade through the front window.

Letkovsky testified that after he arrived at the deli he heard Cisco discuss the plan with Hahn. He described how he drove Hahn to the

Josefsek house and waited in the stopped car while Hahn got out and threw the grenade through the bow window. Both Hahn and Letkovsky testified that each had pled guilty to lesser offenses before the trial began and were awaiting sentencing.

After the district attorney completed the presentation of his proof, the defendant Anthony Cisco testified on his own behalf. According to his version of the events, when Hahn came to work at the deli on May 9, he started drinking beer and continued to do so all evening. Hahn asked if he could take the smoke grenade with him after work—he was going to a party and would like to set it off there. Cisco said he told Hahn that he could take the grenade and showed him how it worked, warning him that the grenade got very hot when exploded.

When customer Bobby DiCarlo came into the deli later in the evening and spoke with Hahn regarding the grenade, Hahn mentioned something about throwing the grenade through the "guy's front window," Cisco claimed, adding that he had no idea what they were talking about and believed they were not serious about doing anything like that. When Letkovsky stopped by the deli to pick up Hahn after work, Cisco said he had no conversation with him about the grenade before he left with Hahn.

Cisco denied telling Hahn to throw the grenade into the Josefsek house. He bore no grudge against John Josefsek, he said, and had nothing to do with kids breaking outdoor furniture at the Josefseks' house in April, despite the prosecutor's claims that he was behind that earlier vandalism. He also denied knowingly selling beer to minors and said no illegal drugs were sold at the deli.

In his testimony, Cisco said that Hahn came to the deli the next day and told him that he had thrown the grenade into the Josefsek house and started the fire. That was the first time he connected the grenade with the fire. He told Hahn to see a lawyer and go to the police and gave the same advice to Letkovsky and Leary when he learned they were with Hahn at the time.

Cisco testified that he was at the deli on the evening of May 12 when two detectives arrived, arrested him and put him in their car. He claimed that he told his wife in the detectives' presence to call his lawyer, Lou England, and when they arrived at the homicide squad headquarters, he demanded that he be allowed to contact his lawyer, which the police denied. In Cisco's recounting, the detectives questioned him about his alleged involvement with the Josefsek house fire, and he never admitted any involvement. The interrogation stopped only when the lawyer from the Siben office called. Cisco's testimony ended the presentation of evidence at the trial.

After closing arguments by O'Leary and Spota, I instructed the jury upon the law. Hahn and Letkovsky were both accomplice witnesses, and the special rule of evidence relating to such witnesses applied in this case. That is, a defendant may not be convicted of a crime upon the testimony of an accomplice unsupported by corroborative evidence tending to connect the defendant with the commission of such crime. I explained to the jury how that rule applied to the evidence. The district attorney had argued that he had presented evidence other than Hahn's and Letkovsky's testimony that tended to connect Cisco with the commission of the crimes: the testimony of neighboring deli owner Frank Bucaria and Tony's Deli customers Jeffrey Hamilton and Matthew Oresky as to their conversations with Cisco at the deli regarding Josefsek, and the testimony of detectives Rafferty and Halverson as to Cisco's oral incriminatory admissions on the evening of May 12. I also instructed the jury as to the laws of conspiracy, arson, and both types of murder charged: felony murder and depraved indifference reckless murder.

The jury returned their verdicts on November 25 after one day's deliberations: guilty as charged of conspiracy, arson, and eight counts of murder (felony murder and depraved indifference murder for each of the four victims). John Josefsek told reporters the verdict "lifted a great weight off my shoulders ... But it won't bring back my family," according to *Newsday*.

I pronounced sentence upon Cisco on January 12, 1981. When interviewed during the presentence investigation and again in his remarks before me, Cisco claimed he was not guilty and placed all the blame upon Andrew Hahn. I sentenced Cisco to indeterminate sentences of imprisonment as follows: one to four years on the conspiracy conviction, five to fifteen years on the arson conviction, and twenty-five years to life on each of the eight murder convictions. I directed that all sentences run concurrently with each other and that Cisco be delivered to the Ossining Correctional Facility.

EPILOGUE

On December 16, 1980, I sentenced Andrew Hahn to a sentence of imprisonment having a maximum of nine years and a minimum of two years. After three years of imprisonment in jail and state prison, Hahn was released on parole on June 13, 1983, and discharged from parole on February 2, 1987. On February 10, 1981, Judge Doyle sentenced Andrew Letkovsky to five years of probation. Such sentence had been recommended by the probation department and Detective Rafferty of the homicide squad.

Anthony Cisco appealed his convictions to the Appellate Division of the Supreme Court in Brooklyn, and on April 27, 1987, four justices of that court affirmed the convictions in a two-page decision.

In 1989 Cisco brought a proceeding in the Supreme Court of Suffolk County seeking to vacate his convictions pursuant to Article 440 of the criminal procedure law. He prepared his own documents alleging several grounds: (1) that the district attorney violated his right to *Rosario* material as to several trial witnesses, and (2) that the district attorney violated his right to due process of law by misleading the jury and defense counsel as to the sentence to be imposed upon Andrew Letkovsky. (The New York Court of Appeals ruled many years ago in the *Rosario* case that when a prosecutor calls a witness upon trial the defendant must be provided with any prior statement/report made or prior testimony by the witness.) After examining the trial record and other documents, I rendered a lengthy decision finding no violation of the *Rosario* rule and no violation of Cisco's due-process rights.

On May 12, 2005, Cisco had served his minimum sentence of twenty-five years and was eligible for release on parole. In parole hearings held in 2005, 2007, and 2009, Cisco still denied any guilt, and release was each time denied. On April 6, 2011, Anthony Cisco died in prison at the age of sixty-nine. His total imprisonment had lasted one week short of thirty-one years.

PART 4

The Drunken Cop
The Jack Sweeney Murder
March 18, 1981

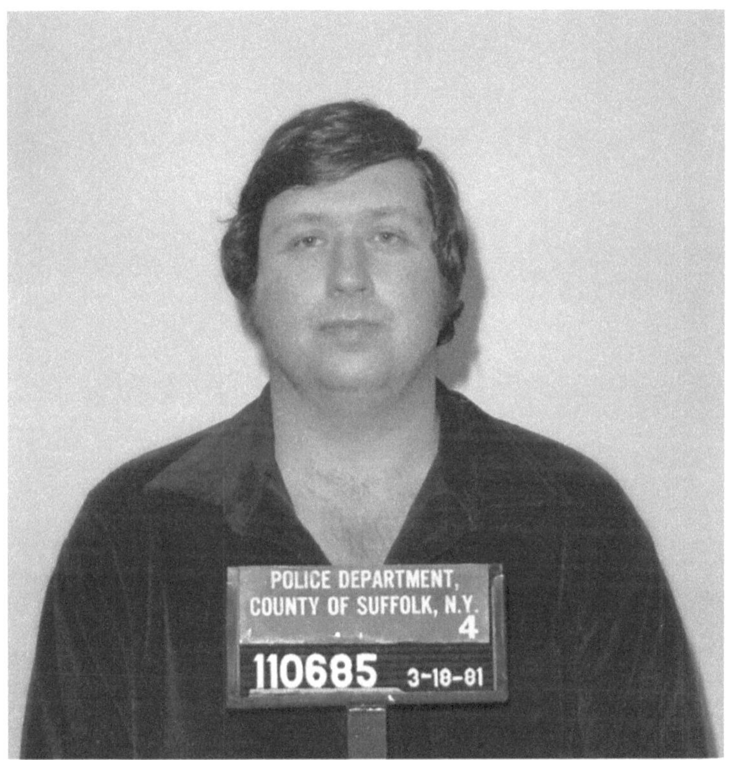

Daniel Gallagher, arrested on March 18, 1981,
for the murder of a fellow police officer

THE ST. PATRICK'S DAY BINGE

In March 1981, Daniel Patrick Gallagher was thirty-one years old and had been a patrolman in the New York City Police Department for ten years. The third child in a Brooklyn Irish-Catholic family, he was a portly man: six feet, five inches tall and weighing well over two hundred pounds. His older brother, Monsignor Thomas Gallagher, was education secretary at the United States Conference of Catholic Bishops in Washington, DC, and his older sister, Marie Gallagher, was a Catholic nun and principal of St. Anselm's parochial school in Brooklyn, where his parents still lived. His younger brother, Robert Gallagher, worked and lived in Georgia. Gallagher and his wife of ten years, Monica, lived in Brentwood in a house at 10 Arlyn Court with their two daughters, aged seven and four. He had been assigned to the 109th precinct in Flushing, Queens for two years.

On March 11, 1981 Gallagher learned he was scheduled to work St. Patrick's Day parade duty in Manhattan and told his wife about the assignment that evening. St. Patrick's Day was originally scheduled to be a day off, and the Gallagher family had already planned their activities. Monica Gallagher was angry about the change and asked her husband to attempt to get his parade duty cancelled. Gallagher spoke to the precinct captain the following day and was told nothing could be done about it.

On St. Patrick's Day morning, Gallagher drove to the park-and-ride lot at the Wicks Road entrance to the Long Island Expressway and parked his car. He met a fellow officer and rode with him to the precinct headquarters in Flushing, where he changed into his uniform. Then he rode with another fellow officer, Joseph Brode, to the police roll-call location at Third Avenue and Eighty-Sixth Street in Manhattan, arriving there at 10:30 a.m.

After mustering in, Gallagher walked to his assigned area of duty—Eighty-Fourth Street between Madison and Park Avenues—to handle traffic at this location. Brode's assigned area was nearby. As later came out in court, Gallagher's personal celebration of his Irish ancestry began within the hour, when he was invited into a Catholic school hall on the block that was being utilized for the day as a canteen by New York City firemen. There he enjoyed a second breakfast of coffee and cake before resuming his post. The firemen invited Gallagher back at about 12:30 p.m., when he partook of a sixteen-ounce container of beer drawn from a tapped keg. After returning to the street, where he stayed for twenty minutes, he went back to the firemen's canteen and had a lunch consisting of three frankfurters and three more beers in the same sixteen-ounce containers.

After lunch, Gallagher resumed his post for a short while before returning yet again to the firemen's canteen, where by 4:00 p.m. he had drunk three more beers. Gallagher then met Brode, and the two walked several blocks east to a Catholic church on Eighty-Fifth Street between First and Second Avenues—the location of the New York City police Holy Name Society canteen. They both had sandwiches and salads, and Gallagher had two scotch and waters.

Gallagher resumed his post until 6:30 p.m., at which time he walked back to the mustering location, where he was dismissed at about 7:00 p.m. After purchasing two bottles of beer in a nearby grocery store, Gallagher rejoined Brode, and they drove back to precinct headquarters in Flushing, with Gallagher consuming the beer en route. Arriving there at 7:45 p.m., they changed out of uniform and drove to the Area Code 212 Restaurant in Whitestone, Queens, arriving at 9:00 p.m.

This restaurant was a favorite of police officers assigned to the 109th precinct, and there were a number of them there at the time. Gallagher and Brode joined other officers at the bar, where they were served beer, and then ordered and ate dinner. After the meal, they were served the drink in honor of the day—Irish coffees containing extra-large shots of

     THOMAS M. STARK

Irish whiskey. Each consumed three. A female friend of Brode's was at the restaurant, and Brode and Gallagher took her home to her apartment in Flushing at 11:30 p.m., where each celebrated the day again with three more Irish coffees.

It was 1:30 a.m. on March 18 before Brode and Gallagher started on the drive back to Suffolk County. Arriving at the park-and-ride lot at Exit 54 on the Long Island Expressway at 2:30 a.m., Gallagher got out of Brode's car and went to his own. Each drove his own car to the nearby Brentwood business district, stopping at the Fife and Drum Tavern on Suffolk Avenue, where the previous evening's St. Patrick's Day party was still in progress. This tavern was popular with New York City Police Department officers who resided in the Brentwood area. It was owned by Michael Grant (a former Suffolk County legislator who also owned and operated the funeral home across the street), and police officers from both New York City and Suffolk County were treated well there.

Brode and Gallagher went into the bar area, and Gallagher had a bottle of ale. Brode noticed New York City Police Department friends seated at a table, and he and Gallagher joined them. They were Patrolman David McAteer and his wife Carol and Sergeant Jack Sweeney and his wife Kathleen. Sweeney, a thirty-nine-year-old father of four, was assigned to the 100th Precinct in Rockaway, Queens. Gallagher knew the McAteers, and Brode introduced him to the Sweeneys, whom he had never met before.

The McAteers and Kathleen Sweeney had been at the Fife and Drum since 11:00 p.m., and Jack Sweeney had joined them at 2:30 a.m. after getting off duty. The group socialized until the restaurant announced "last call" at 3:15 a.m. McAteer invited all of them to his house but announced he had little liquor in stock, so it was B.Y.O.B. All six left the Fife and Drum at 3:30 a.m. in their own cars. Both Sweeney and Gallagher stopped at an all-night convenience store and picked up a number of six-packs of beer. The McAteers lived at 119 Dolce Street in Brentwood, and Gallagher, Brode, and the Sweeneys all arrived there by 4:00 a.m. Brode had had enough by 4:30 a.m. and left for home.

Kathleen Sweeney called it a night at 5:00 a.m. and drove home, while Carol McAteer went up to bed.

McAteer, Sweeney, and Gallagher continued emptying the six-packs until McAteer realized that his son had missed the school bus and would have to be driven to school. All three—plus the son—piled into McAteer's two-door Oldsmobile Cutlass and dropped the boy off at his school, St. John the Baptist Diocesan High School in West Islip. Sweeney then invited McAteer and Gallagher to his house. He lived at 11 Circle Drive in Bay Shore, and the three arrived there at 8:45 a.m. While Kathleen Sweeney was in her bedroom sleeping, the three men sat at the kitchen table drinking beer. McAteer had had enough to drink and made himself coffee, calling his wife at 9:00 a.m. to let her know he and Gallagher were at Sweeney's house.

In the meantime, Monica Gallagher was somewhat frantic. Her husband hadn't come home the night before, and she didn't know where he was—he had not called since he left to go to work the previous day. She called Joe Brode, and he told her he had last seen Gallagher at the McAteer's house. She then called Carol McAteer, who told her she had just learned her husband and Gallagher were at the Sweeney's house in Bay Shore and gave her the telephone number. When Monica called there, Sweeney answered and gave the phone to Gallagher.

Monica told her husband that she was furious with him over his conduct—that he could just come home, pack his bags and get out—and then hung up. Gallagher returned to the kitchen table, upset and embarrassed that his wife had called him at Sweeney's house to check up on him. A drowsy McAteer fell asleep in his chair, while Sweeney and Gallagher were now drinking wine from a two-liter jug, all the beer having been consumed. McAteer woke up about 10:45 a.m. and called his wife again, telling her he was leaving in a few minutes and on his way home, taking Sweeney and Gallagher to pick up their cars, which they had left parked near the McAteer house. Sweeney told his wife, who was now awake, that he was going to pick up his car and would be back.

All three men got into McAteer's coupe, with Sweeney sitting in the right side of the rear seats, Gallagher sitting in the front passenger's seat, and McAteer driving. They got to the McAteer house at 11:15 a.m., and McAteer, seeing that both Sweeney and Gallagher were too intoxicated to drive their own cars home, decided to drive each of them home instead. He told them that he was taking them home, and they or their wives could pick up their cars later. Not knowing Gallagher's address, McAteer asked him and learned it was on a street off Commack Road just before the St. Joseph Convent's cemetery.

While driving northwest on Commack Road, McAteer realized he had passed the street leading to Gallagher's street and made a U-turn at the next intersection. Just as McAteer was preparing to turn left off Commack Road, Gallagher suddenly reached down with his right arm to his left ankle holster and withdrew his off-duty weapon, a Smith & Wesson .38-caliber five-shot revolver. He turned his body to the left, facing the rear seat, and fired three shots in rapid succession toward Sweeney. One shot missed and two shots struck Sweeney, one in the neck and one in the chest.

The loud noise of the weapon's discharge startled McAteer, who looked to his right and saw Gallagher holding the revolver. What ensued was a brief struggle for the gun. Calling out, "Danny, Danny, what are you doing?," McAteer let go of the steering wheel and put both hands around Gallagher's hand that held the gun, at the same time applying the brakes as hard as he could. The car veered to the right and stopped with the right wheels up on the sidewalk and the left wheels still in Commack Road. Gallagher released his grip on the revolver, and McAteer took it from him. McAteer got out of the car and ran to the other side. Gallagher had gotten out of the car and was standing next to the open door.

McAteer pulled the back of the front passenger seat forward calling to Sweeney, who made no response. Sweeney was leaning forward, and McAteer could see blood stains on his chest. McAteer pushed him back upright to prevent blood accumulating in the upper chest and drowning him. A neighbor had heard the gunshots and came to the car. McAteer asked him to call 911 and tell them to send an ambulance—a police officer had been shot. He noticed at this time that a woman had come to the car and was taking Gallagher to a house on the other side of Commack Road. He attempted to remove Sweeney from the car but was unable to because Sweeney was a big man—six feet tall and weighing over two hundred pounds. McAteer saw that Sweeney was not breathing and was probably dead.

"I'M FINISHED. I PANICKED."

Purely by happenstance, at the time of the shooting Monica Gallagher was about to enter Barbara Traola's house on Commack Road. Monica had been out with Traola during the morning and was going to have lunch with her. Alerted by the sound of gunshots, she noticed the McAteer car stopped over the curb on the opposite side of the road. She heard McAteer shout, "Danny!" at a man standing next to the car door and recognized him as her husband. Running to the car, she reached her husband, who said something about how they were going to kill him and begged her to get him away from there. She took her husband to the Traola house, where she seated him on the couch in the family room.

In the meanwhile, as a result of a police radio call at 11:52 a.m. reporting an accident at Lloyd Drive and Commack Road, two Suffolk County police officers on sector car duty in the Brentwood area— Patrolman Henry Stewart in one vehicle and Sergeant Edward Holmes in another—headed to that location. While on their way, a further radio call reported that a police officer had been shot at the scene of the accident. Upon Stewart and Holmes's arrival at the scene, McAteer identified himself as a police officer and told them that fellow police officer Daniel Gallagher had shot the third police officer in the car and was now at a house that he pointed to across Commack Road.

By this time, an ambulance was at the scene, and emergency medical technicians were attending to Sweeney in the rear seat of the car. Holmes and Stewart crossed the street to the Traola house and were admitted by Barbara Traola and directed to the family room, where they found Gallagher and his wife seated on the couch. Holmes told Stewart to place Gallagher under arrest and advise him of his Miranda rights. Crouching down in front of Gallagher, Stewart said he was placing him under arrest and read him his Miranda rights. Gallagher responded that he understood his rights and told Stewart he did not need a lawyer. Asked by Holmes where he had been, Gallagher said he had worked the parade the day before, gone out that night drinking, and met up with McAteer and Sweeney and that they had been drinking all night. After Gallagher's wife got up from the couch and went away for a few moments, Gallagher motioned to Holmes and Stewart to come closer and said to them, "I'm going to die … They're going to get me. If not today then tomorrow, so I went the whole nine yards."

While this was going on, Sweeney had been taken by ambulance to Southside Hospital in Bay Shore, where he had been pronounced dead. The police homicide squad had been notified, and two homicide detectives, Kenneth McGuire and James Cassidy, had been sent to the scene in Brentwood. They were advised by Holmes as to what had occurred and that Gallagher was at the Traola house in Stewart's custody. McGuire and Cassidy went to the family room of the Traola house and told Gallagher he was being taken to homicide squad headquarters in Hauppauge and gave the same information to his wife. Gallagher was escorted out of the house by McGuire, Stewart, and Cassidy and taken to the homicide squad in an unmarked vehicle.

En route to Hauppauge, Cassidy told Gallagher his Miranda rights. Gallagher said the cop had already advised him of his rights and that he understood them and was willing to talk to them without a lawyer. Cassidy asked him to tell them what happened, and Gallagher responded, "I'm in big trouble, I'm finished, I pumped the guy. … I panicked. I thought it was a hit. They were going to hit me … if not today, they would hit me tomorrow."

When they arrived at squad headquarters, Gallagher was further questioned by McGuire and Cassidy. He admitted that he shot Sweeney a couple of times. When describing the shooting, Gallagher demonstrated how he had removed his revolver with his right hand from his ankle holster, raised the weapon, turned to his left and fired into the rear seat. When asked, Gallagher said he was willing to give a written statement, and Cassidy prepared one incorporating what he had told them. The statement read as follows: "On 3/18/81 I was with two other city cops. I don't know their names. We were drinking. I started drinking beer and scotch. I started drinking after work. I was partying because it was St. Paddy's day. I was drunk. I don't remember too much. I was scared. I believed the cop with me was going to kill me. I believed it was a fucken [sic] hit. I panicked pulled my gun and shot him twice."

After reading the written statement, Gallagher said he would not sign it without consulting with a lawyer and told Cassidy he now wanted to speak with a lawyer. At this point all questioning of Gallagher stopped. A few minutes later an attorney from Richard Hartman's office representing the Police Benevolent Association called and asked that all questioning of New York City police officers be stopped. Later Gallagher was permitted to speak to two attorneys from Hartman's office and a representative from the New York City Police Benevolent Association. Gallagher agreed that a sample of his blood be taken for analysis, and this was done at 3:50 p.m. The test showed the presence of ethyl alcohol at a concentration of 0.19 percent. At 5:00 p.m., Gallagher was transferred to the nearby Fourth Precinct for prints and detention.

A SURPRISING ADMISSION

On March 20, bail of $10,000 was fixed, and Gallagher was released from jail after it was posted. Over the next several days, the district attorney's office presented the case to the grand jury. On March 23, the grand jury filed an indictment accusing Daniel Gallagher of two counts of murder in the second degree—one count of intentional murder of Jack Sweeney and one count of depraved indifference reckless murder of Jack Sweeney. Gallagher was arraigned on the indictment before Judge Robert W. Doyle of the County Court on the same day. He was represented by attorney Edward M. Rappaport of New York City, who had been retained by the New York City Police Benevolent Association. During the next five months the defendant's attorney and the assistant district attorney assigned to try the case, Edward C. Jablonski, deputy chief of the major offense bureau, were engaged in voluntary disclosure of evidence. Rappaport advised the district attorney that the defendant intended to raise the defense of involuntary intoxication at trial and provided the names of several expert witnesses he intended to call to testify in connection with such defense.

Because of Judge Doyle's busy trial schedule, on September 14, 1981, the county administrative judge transferred the case to the Criminal Term of the Supreme Court, where I was presiding. On September 23, Rappaport and Jablonski appeared before me and argued several pretrial motions brought by the defendant, which I decided a week later. Rappaport had moved to suppress the oral statements Gallagher made to the police after his arrest, and I conducted a two-day hearing on the motion on October 19 and 20, rendering a decision on October 26, finding that there had been no violation of Gallagher's rights under the Fifth Amendment to the Constitution. Gallagher's trial began before me on October 26 with jury selection and ended with the jury's verdict five weeks later on December 2.

Forty-four witnesses testified, and twenty-four items were put into evidence as exhibits. The jury consisted of ten men and two women, with three men and one woman as alternate jurors. Jablonski's opening statement to the jury recounted the events of March 17 and 18, beginning at the Fife and Drum Tavern and continuing through Gallagher's fatal shooting of Sweeney and his statements at the Traola house and the homicide squad headquarters.

Rappaport's opening statement was quite out of the ordinary. He admitted that Gallagher shot Sweeney and caused his death. He related in detail Gallagher's life history: his youth in Brooklyn, his education, his religion, his employment as a New York City police officer, his marriage, and the birth of his two children. Then he recounted in detail the sequence of his drinking (drink by drink), starting during Gallagher's St. Patrick's Day parade duty and continuing in Flushing, Whitestone, the Fife and Drum Tavern in Brentwood, the McAteer house, and the Sweeney house.

Rappaport told the jury that Gallagher was forced to drink wine by Sweeney, and that Sweeney placed a lighted marijuana cigarette between Gallagher's lips and forced him to inhale the smoke. Gallagher recalled nothing from then on, being in a psychotic mental blackout. He next remembered being in a car hearing a strange voice and experiencing abnormal sensations. He had no recollection of the shooting itself or his statements to the police.

The jury would hear the testimony of several expert doctors who would describe Gallagher's mental condition at the time of the shooting—extreme alcoholic intoxication and cannabis intoxication—Rappaport said. Because of his condition, the lawyer argued, Gallagher could form no criminal intent at the time he shot Sweeney, and his actions in drawing and firing his gun at Sweeney were involuntary acts for which he was not criminally responsible.

As the trial got underway, David McAteer was the witness who recounted the basic facts of the case: the events at the Fife and Drum Tavern, when Gallagher joined their group and met the Sweeneys for the first time; the events at his house after the tavern closed; what happened at the Sweeney house; the shooting of Sweeney by Gallagher in McAteer's moving car in Brentwood; and the aftermath. Joseph Brode testified regarding his and Gallagher's activities at the St. Patrick's Day parade in Manhattan and their activities thereafter in Flushing and Whitestone before returning to Suffolk County and ending up at the Fife and Drum Tavern.

The Suffolk County police officers who investigated the shooting and interrogated Gallagher testified, telling the jury the contents of Gallagher's oral statements made that afternoon and describing his condition at that time. Monica Gallagher testified about her attempts to locate her husband the morning of March 18, how she happened to be within earshot of the shooting a few blocks from her home, how she took her husband from McAteer's car to the Traola house, and his statements to her before the police arrived.

Dr. John Grauerholz, Suffolk County deputy medical examiner, testified about his autopsy of the body of Jack Sweeney, the internal injuries caused by the two bullets, and the cause of death. He also testified that Sweeney was extremely intoxicated when he died, having a blood alcohol content of 0.21 percent. The two intact bullets found in Sweeney's body at the autopsy were examined by Detective Alfred Della Penna, senior firearms examiner of the police laboratory, and he testified that he found them to have been fired from Gallagher's .38-caliber off-duty revolver.

During the testimony of another Suffolk County police officer, Robert Kellenberger, I made an interesting evidence ruling. McAteer had testified before the grand jury that before the shooting, during the trip to Gallagher's house, he heard Sweeney and Gallagher conversing but wasn't paying close attention to what they were saying. On trial he testified that he heard no disagreements or arguments between Gallagher and Sweeney before the shooting—in fact, he wasn't able to hear *any* remarks between them on the trip to Gallagher's house.

Officer Kellenberger had responded to the scene of the shooting, and after officers Stewart and Holmes had left to go into the Traola house, he asked McAteer what had happened in the car. McAteer told him that just before the shooting Sweeney and Gallagher had been arguing. When Kellenberger testified that McAteer had heard an argument just before the shooting, Rappaport objected, claiming that the district attorney was attempting to impeach McAteer, his own witness. I sustained the objection and directed that Kellenberger's testimony as to what McAteer told him about hearing an argument be stricken. I have often pondered the situation where a judge directs a jury to disregard testimony they have heard but is thereafter stricken. Do the jurors actually put it out of their minds and not let it in any way influence their ultimate deliberations?

AN UNORTHODOX DEFENSE

Rappaport began the defendant's case by calling twenty-two character witnesses to the stand. They included two Catholic priests, four Catholic sisters, twelve New York City police officers, and four of Gallagher's neighbors. Each testified that Daniel Gallagher's reputation for peacefulness, caution, calmness, truthfulness, and honesty was good. Evidence of a defendant's good reputation, if believed, is not a defense to the commission of a crime. Such evidence is but one fact, taken together with all the other evidence in a case, which a jury must consider in reaching its ultimate conclusion of guilt or innocence. If a defendant's good reputation, combined with all the evidence in the case, raises a reasonable doubt as to guilt, then the defendant must be found not guilty. Conversely, if a jury is convinced that guilt has been proven beyond a reasonable doubt, a jury must convict, notwithstanding a defendant's good reputation.

Gallagher testified on his own behalf. He described how he was assigned parade duty in Manhattan on St. Patrick's Day and his unsuccessful attempt to change the assignment. And he chronicled his two days of drinking: during respites from parade duty at the fireman's and the Holy Name Society's canteens; on the way back to precinct headquarters in Flushing after finishing duty; at the Area Code 212 Restaurant, Brode's girlfriend's apartment, and the Fife and Drum Tavern in Brentwood that night; and at the McAteer house and then the Sweeney house on the morning of March 18.

Gallagher testified that when the beer ran out at Sweeney's house (McAteer was by then asleep on a kitchen chair), Sweeney brought out a jug of red wine and poured a glass for him. Gallagher said he didn't like wine and told Sweeney so, but Sweeney insisted that he drink it. He drank three glasses only upon Sweeney's urging. After finishing the wine, he began to feel terrible, he said. He had never felt like this before. Everything seemed woozy.

At this point, Gallagher recalled Sweeney leaving the kitchen and returning with a tray of marijuana cigarettes and saying, "Now the party will really start." Sweeney told him to take one and he refused, Gallagher said, whereupon Sweeney lit one and tried to hand it to him. As he continued to resist taking it, Sweeney put the cigarette into his mouth and forced him to inhale the smoke.

Gallagher said that he didn't remember any of the events thereafter until he recalled being in a car in the front seat with McAteer and hearing a strange voice from the rear saying, "Can we trust this guy? Is he going to be any problem for us? Will we have any problem with him at all?" Then someone hit him in the back of the neck with an open hand, he said, and he next recalled standing outside of the car, seeing his wife there, and yelling, "Someone is going to kill me—get me out of here."

The next thing Gallagher remembered was being stuck in the arm with a needle (the drawing of blood for the alcohol test later that afternoon). He said he did not recall being in the Traola house or being given the Miranda warnings or riding to the homicide squad headquarters or being questioned by the police or his alleged statements, both oral and written. Gallagher testified that he did not remember any other events occurring while riding in McAteer's car that morning, including the shooting of Sweeney.

Gallagher's testimony about Sweeney bringing out a tray of marijuana cigarettes and forcing him to smoke one created a big issue of fact in the trial. Kathleen Sweeney testified that there was no marijuana in her home and that her husband never possessed the drug and to her knowledge never smoked it. McAteer testified that he was familiar with the odor of marijuana smoke and did not smell it in Sweeney's house that morning when he decided to take Gallagher and Sweeney back to their cars.

During the balance of the trial, the jury heard expert testimony presented by six doctors, four called by Rappaport and two by Jablonski, each expressing opinions as to Gallagher's mental and physical condition prior to and at the time of the shooting. The four called by Rappaport for the defense were Dr. Dominick DiMaio, a forensic pathologist; Dr. Michael Peterson, a psychiatrist; Dr. Daniel Schwartz, a forensic psychiatrist; and Dr. Sidney Cohen, a psycho-pharmacologist. The two called by Jablonski were Dr. Harold Zolan, a forensic psychiatrist, and Dr. Bernard Salzman, a psychiatrist.

DiMaio said he had examined the report of Sweeney's autopsy and the evidence as to the degree of Gallagher's intoxication after his arrest. Given a blood alcohol reading of .19 percent at 4:00 p.m. on March 18, he was of the opinion that Gallagher's blood alcohol reading at 11:00 a.m. when he stopped drinking would have been .29 percent, a level reached after having consumed at least twenty-five drinks. The other three doctors who testified for the defendant, Peterson, Schwartz, and Cohen, examined Gallagher on various dates between September 18, 1981, and November 7, 1981. Gallagher told each of them that Sweeney had forced him to drink wine and take several puffs of a marijuana cigarette on the morning of March 18, and each doctor assumed the truth of this in forming his opinion as to Gallagher's condition at the time of the shooting. Each doctor was also told the extent of Gallagher's consumption of alcohol during a nearly twenty-four-hour period and his state of intoxication at the end of that period.

The opinions expressed by the three doctors as to Gallagher's condition at the time of the shooting were similar: his extreme intoxication resulted in an inability to exercise his mental capacity; the marijuana enhanced the effect of the intoxication to bring on a paranoid psychotic condition; that in this condition reaching for his revolver and shooting Sweeney were involuntary and not the result of a conscious effort; that he was blacked out for a time, and that accounted for his present lack of memory as to certain of that morning's events; and that because of his condition he could not form an intent to commit a crime when he shot Sweeney.

Upon the completion of the doctors' testimony, Rappaport rested Gallagher's case. Jablonski then presented the district attorney's case in rebuttal. Doctors Zolan and Salzman testified that each had examined Gallagher on October 5, 1981, and October 13, 1981, respectively.

Gallagher told both of being forced by Sweeney to drink wine and take several puffs of marijuana smoke, and both assumed that Gallagher did in fact take the puffs of marijuana. But neither believed he was forced to do so. Zolan testified that in his opinion Gallagher was reluctant to drink the wine and smoke marijuana but did so of his own volition upon Sweeney's urging. Both doctors felt that this minor inhalation of marijuana smoke could not have caused any blackout or loss of memory, pointing to the fact that Gallagher, shortly after the shooting, even though still intoxicated, was able to give the police a detailed and coherent account of the events in the car and demonstrate how he drew his revolver, turned, and shot Sweeney.

Both Zolan and Salzman shared the view that Gallagher was not in a psychotic state. His actions in the car were voluntary, and he intended to shoot Sweeney, even to kill him. Zolan testified that he believed Gallagher was now fabricating his claim that he could not remember any of the facts of the shooting. In both doctors' opinions, Gallagher's intoxication was caused by his own decision to consume all the liquor, beer, and wine he did from the morning of March 17 to the morning of March 18, and that no one forced him to do so. Zolan believed that Gallagher's expressions of fear after the shooting that others wanted to kill him were caused by his extreme intoxication.

Both Rappaport and Jablonski rested their proof, and each made lengthy summations to the jury. I then instructed the jury as to all matters of law that applied to the case, including the elements of both types of murder charged: intentional murder and depraved indifference reckless murder and the alternative lesser included offenses of both. I also explained that Gallagher's voluntary intoxication did not excuse his commission of the crimes but may be considered by them as negating the intentional element of the crime if the intoxication was extreme enough to do so.

As to Gallagher's defense of involuntary intoxication, based on his claim that the wine and marijuana smoke inhalation were forced on him by Sweeney, I gave a lengthy instruction on the law that applies to this defense. On December 2, 1981, after deliberating for ten hours over two days, the jury convicted Gallagher of intentional murder as charged and manslaughter in the second degree, a lesser included offense of depraved indifference reckless murder. The *Newsday* story about the verdict noted that Gallagher showed no emotion, while "his mother, Emma Gallagher, collapsed in tears … his wife, Monica, in a front row, closed her eyes for a long moment, and then fought back sobs. Outside the courtroom,

Gallagher's father, Thomas, put his face in his hands and wept openly." A "shaken" Kathleen Sweeney said, "Nobody wins."

The murder conviction required by law that I confine Gallagher, and I committed him to the custody of the sheriff to await sentencing and ordered a presentence investigation.

POWERFUL APPEALS

Before Gallagher's sentencing, I received more than six hundred letters urging me to impose a lenient sentence—it was easily the largest outpouring of support for any convicted defendant who had appeared before me. A great majority of the writers did not know Gallagher personally but were asked to write to me by his brother, Monsignor Thomas Gallagher, his sister, Sister Marie Vianney, and his parents. The most unusual of the letters were those from seven bishops of the Roman Catholic Church: Bishops McGann, Daly, and Ryan of the Rockville Centre Diocese, Bishop Curtis of the Bridgeport Diocese, Bishop Pilarczyk of the Cincinnati Diocese, Bishop Kelly of the U.S. Conference of Catholic Bishops, and Cardinal Bernardin of Cincinnati.

On February 2, 1982, Gallagher appeared before me for sentencing. After summarizing the factors that I had considered in determining a just and proper sentence, I imposed a life sentence of imprisonment with a minimum period of fifteen years on the murder conviction and a sentence of imprisonment of four to twelve years on the manslaughter conviction and directed both sentences to run concurrent with each other, less than the sentence the district attorney had requested. Press reports noted that Gallagher was heard to murmur, "I'm sorry," as the sentence was passed down.

I then directed that Gallagher be delivered to the Ossining Correctional Facility in upstate New York. State correctional officials had to make a delicate decision in placing Gallagher, a police officer, in an appropriate location in the prison system, considering the attitude of most prisoners toward the police.

Gallagher appealed his conviction to the Appellate Division of the Supreme Court in Brooklyn, his appeal attorney being Nathan R. Sobel of Brooklyn, a former justice of the Supreme Court and Kings County Surrogate Court. Chief Appellate Attorney Mark D. Cohen represented the district attorney. That court rendered its decision on April 14, 1986, with the majority, with one justice dissenting, affirming the murder conviction and modifying the judgment by dismissing the manslaughter conviction in the interest of justice.

The principal legal issue before the appellate court was whether the two murder counts of the indictment should have been submitted to the jury in the alternative, not together, as I did at trial. Interpreting case law and the criminal procedure statute the majority held that they should not have, while the dissenting justice held that they should have. To obtain a final determination of this issue, Gallagher appealed the Appellate Division decision to the New York Court of Appeals in Albany.

That court rendered its decision on May 7, 1987, reversing the Appellate Division and holding that the two murder counts should have been submitted to the jury in the alternative and remitting the case to the Supreme Court of Suffolk County for a new trial on the murder charges. The decision read, in part, "The act [of shooting a person] is either intended or not intended; it cannot simultaneously be both … The two second degree murder counts in the present indictment—intentional murder and depraved mind murder—are inconsistent counts because guilt of one necessarily negates guilt of the other." Gallagher was released from prison after this decision to await a new trial, and the case was assigned to Judge Paul T. D'Amaro.

Gallagher commenced plea bargaining with the district attorney, rather than face a new trial and risk being convicted of murder again (either intentional murder or depraved indifference reckless murder, the latter being much more likely because the prosecution did not have to prove an intent to kill Sweeney for a conviction of that type of murder). This resulted in a plea bargain that was very favorable to Gallagher—a plea of guilty to manslaughter in the second degree, a much lesser degree of homicide than murder, and a sentence of imprisonment of four to twelve years.

In the fall of 1987, Judge D'Amaro approved the plea bargain. Gallagher pled guilty and was sentenced according to the bargain. He was returned to state prison, where he immediately applied to be released on parole. He was parole eligible because he had been imprisoned a total of five years and six months since his conviction on December 2, 1981, and thus he had served his newly imposed four-year minimum sentence. The Parole Board released Gallagher on parole on December 14, 1987, and he remained under parole supervision until January 26, 1991, when he was discharged.

EPILOGUE

The senseless killing of Jack Sweeney by Daniel Gallagher was a tragedy for both families. It came about after gross abuse of drinking of alcoholic beverages by both killer and victim. Sweeney's death left a young widow and four children with a sudden and unexpected loss of a beloved husband and father. Gallagher was dismissed from the New York City Police Department, the shame of his crime being borne by his extended family, and his two children had to grow up with the knowledge of the terrible thing their father had done.

As a result of the shooting, the New York City Police Department adopted stricter regulations concerning the consumption of alcoholic beverages by police officers while on duty. Around the same time, the department changed a regulation requiring officers to carry their firearms even while off duty. The New York City Police Benevolent Association expended a large amount of money in Gallagher's defense—attorney's fees, expert witnesses, and printing the record for the appeal—all somewhat ironic, considering the nature of his crime: the killing of a fellow police officer.

PART 5

A Trio of Memorable Cases

Judge Stark left behind recollections of many other trials that he presided over during his thirty-seven years on the bench. The following three stand out, but for much different reasons. The first, the case of Peter Bartolomeo, is most notable for the legal ruling that followed.

THE PANICKED BURGLAR

The John McLoughlin Murder
April 15, 1978

In the spring of 1979, I presided over a murder trial, *People v. Peter Bartolomeo*, which, after subsequent appeals, established a new rule of law concerning a suspect's state constitutional right to counsel prior to police interrogation, a rule that was in effect for only nine years.

While this rule of law was well known, the story behind it is less so. It's the story of a nineteen-year-old committing his first crime, a house burglary, who panics when he encounters an occupant and shoots and kills the just-awakened victim.

At about 10:00 p.m. on April 14, 1978, Peter Bartolomeo and his friend Joseph Caprisecca met at the Finish Line bar in Deer Park, Long Island. Bartolomeo had with him a loaded .22-caliber semiautomatic pistol, which he had purchased for $100 several weeks earlier. When Bartolomeo told Caprisecca he needed money and was looking for a score, Caprisecca said he knew of a place where there was money and guns. They decided to take Bartolomeo's 1966 Volkswagen, which was light blue with horizontal black stripes on each side. The left tail light was broken, and there was a painted white flange on the right rear wheel. With Bartolomeo driving, the pair headed to Dix Hills, passing the house located at 9 Otsego Avenue, which Caprisecca had burglarized in January. Noticing people and cars at the house, they returned to the bar and shot pool, remaining there until 12:15 a.m.

Driving again to the Dix Hills house, Caprisecca knocked on the front door and rang the bell with no response. One of the occupants, John McLoughlin, was sleeping upstairs, and because of a hearing problem did not hear the doorbell or knocking. The men parked the car a short distance away and entered the house through the unlocked front door. Carpisecca searched downstairs for property to steal while Bartolomeo went upstairs and kicked open a locked bedroom door. Aroused by the noise, McLoughlin got out of bed and confronted Bartolomeo, who drew his pistol and fired five shots in rapid succession. McLoughlin, mortally wounded with four gunshot wounds, fell to the floor. Bartolomeo fled from the house, meeting Caprisecca, who had heard the gunfire, outside. Running to the car, they drove away at high speed.

Unbeknown to Bartolomeo and Caprisecca, two neighborhood teenagers were watching the men from an upstairs bedroom in a nearby house. Angelo and Rose Poukamissas had seen the Volkswagen being parked, the two men walking to the house and returning a few minutes later, and the car leaving very fast. They had an excellent view of the Volkswagen, observing its color, the black stripes, the broken taillight, and the white wheel flange.

After getting into the car, Bartolomeo told Caprisecca of the shooting, saying that he had "blown that motherfucker away." They drove to the public dock in Babylon and threw the pistol well out into the Great South Bay (where police divers later recovered it). Returning to the Finish Line at about 1:00 a.m., Bartolomeo joined a friend, Stephen Manteiga, and confided in him about the shooting, while Caprisecca went home.

The Suffolk County police homicide squad began its investigation with few leads other than the description of the car and the men. In early June, after a car matching it was seen in Deer Park, Bartolomeo became a suspect, and officers began surveillance of his family home. Just before then, on May 27, Bartolomeo had been arrested and, along with Caprisecca, charged with the burglary and arson of another house in Deer Park.

On June 4, Caprisecca was picked up and questioned. He gave the police a written statement, incriminating himself in the McLoughlin burglary and identifying his accomplice, Peter Bartolomeo, as the person who shot and killed McLoughlin. Surveillance of the Bartolomeo house continued, and on the morning of June 5, police officers followed Bartolomeo and his father, Joseph, as they drove from the house. Stopping the car, homicide squad detectives took Peter Bartolomeo into custody and drove to police headquarters in Yaphank with Joseph Bartolomeo following. Bartolomeo was taken to the homicide squad office while his father waited in the lobby. The two detectives who had interrogated Caprisecca the prior evening began to question him.

Informed that Caprisecca had fully implicated him in the murder, Bartolomeo replied, "Bullshit—I had nothing to do with it." Told that his car had been seen at the crime scene, he responded, "Maybe I went for a ride, but I never went in. I didn't hurt anyone." After the police said they had witnesses who saw him going into the house, he said, "I never went upstairs. If anyone got hurt, he must have done it." When police suggested he entered the house with a gun, Bartolomeo said, "Maybe I had a piece, but I never used it. If anyone got hurt, it must have been Joey that did it."

At this point, the interrogation stopped as an attorney had called and requested no further questioning without his presence. Prior to and while the homicide squad detectives were questioning Bartolomeo, they were aware of his recent burglary and arson arrest, but they had no knowledge of whether he had an attorney representing him on those charges. Before trial, Bartolomeo moved to suppress the brief oral statements made to the detectives, and I conducted a six-day hearing on admissibility. Applying settled case law, I ruled that Bartolomeo's oral statements were admissible, even though the detectives were aware of his burglary/arson arrest.

The sixteen-day jury trial started on March 26, 1979. Caprisecca had made a guilty plea bargain with the district attorney and agreed to testify in Bartolomeo's trial in return for leniency in sentencing. His testimony, describing in detail his and Bartolomeo's participation in the burglary and felony murder, was that of an accomplice, and the law required corroboration by other evidence tending to connect Bartolomeo with the crime. Such evidence was amply provided, including the Poukamissas' testimony of seeing the Volkswagen and the two men on the street outside their home and subsequently identifying that Volkswagen. James McKendrick and Ralph Giordano testified about Bartolomeo's purchase of the pistol used in the slaying. Mantiega and McKendrick told the jury about Bartolomeo's incriminating statements after the crime, and the two homicide squad detectives recounted Bartolomeo's oral statements before his attorney called. Bartolomeo's defense at trial was an alibi, calling several witnesses who said he had never left the Finish Line that evening and that Caprisecca's trial testimony was false, given in an attempt to shift the blame for the murder.

The jury found Bartolomeo guilty of felony murder, and on May 22, I sentenced him to life imprisonment, with a minimum of twenty years. His conviction was affirmed by the Appellate Division of the Supreme Court on July 21, 1980, and he was granted leave to appeal to the New York Court of Appeals.

Before the Bartolomeo case reached the Court of Appeals, that court decided *People v. Rogers*, which set aside prior case holdings to the contrary and held that if the police know that a suspect is represented by an attorney in an unrelated case, the suspect may not waive his Miranda rights and consent to be questioned without the presence of his attorney. In deciding the Bartolomeo appeal on June 16, 1981, the Court of Appeals applied *Rogers* retroactively. And the court went a step further, holding that if the police know that a suspect is a defendant in an unrelated case, they have a duty to inquire of the suspect whether he has an attorney in the unrelated case. Failing to do so, they are charged with knowledge of the attorney's representation, and, applying the *Rogers* rule, the suspect may not waive his Miranda rights and consent to be questioned without the presence of his attorney. Applying this new rule to Bartolomeo, the court reversed the conviction and directed a new trial.

Suffolk County District Attorney Patrick Henry called the ruling "possibly the worst decision in the history of criminal law in New York," the *New York Times* reported. "It goes far beyond what the United States

Supreme Court requires to protect the rights of an accused criminal." One of the dissenting appeals judges said the rule carried the right to counsel to "to unheard-of extremes."

The second trial, with Bartolomeo represented by new attorneys, began before me on January 5, 1982, and after 21 days Bartolomeo was again convicted of felony murder. I again imposed a sentence of twenty years to life. The same evidence was used against him—except his oral admissions to the police. Those brief admissions were minuscule compared to the other overwhelming evidence of his guilt. His second conviction was affirmed by the Appellate Division on March 30, 1987, and leave to appeal to the Court of Appeals was denied.

In the meanwhile, the new Bartolomeo rule had to be applied to criminal cases statewide and caused great confusion. On July 2, 1990, the Court of Appeals abolished the Bartolomeo rule by a 4 to 3 vote, and this short-lived and controversial rule passed into criminal history.

Long Island has been home to countless political scandals over the decades. In the early 1970s, Judge Stark played a small part in a memorable Suffolk County one.

THE PUGNACIOUS POL

The Fred Fellman Case
May to July 1971

In the spring of 1971, I heard a quite interesting non-jury criminal trial, the *People v. Anthony Serigano*. After a three-year *Newsday* investigation and exposé of the so-called "Suffolk scandals" involving Republican party leaders and others in the town of Babylon, the Suffolk County District Attorney's office, led by Chief Assistant District Attorney Maurice Nadjari, obtained several indictments. One involved Fred Fellman, the young, pugnacious leader of the Babylon Town Republican Committee and Republican Club. Along with Anthony Serigano, Babylon's sanitation director, and Richard DiNapoli, the town's recreation director, Fellman was charged with grand larceny in the theft of party monies.

Serigano and DiNapoli had both worked on the 1968 election campaign, and under the organization's by-laws they could not be compensated from party funds. To get around this restriction, the trio gave a local printer Republican Club checks totaling $2,700, purportedly in payment of a bill. The printer, in turn, delivered his own checks—$1,000 each to Serigano and DiNapoli and $700 to Fellman. Another indictment charged Fellman alone with stealing club funds by making out checks to employees for "overtime" and having the employees cash the checks and give him the cash.

The books and records of the committee and club were placed into evidence, and I was flabbergasted with what they disclosed. During the three-year period of Fellman's leadership, practically all of his and his associates' meals and personal expenses were paid using the American Express cards of the committee and the club. Donations to charities, purportedly from Fellman, were made from party funds. The same grand jury that indicted Fellman, Serigano and DiNapoli separately charged Fellman with grand larceny in the purchase of new trailers for the Babylon mobile home park that he managed. The scheme involved the manufacturer inflating the bill by several hundred dollars and Fellman pocketing the difference.

Serigano's case was severed and tried by me without a jury in July 1971. It was a short trial, and after finding Serigano guilty I imposed a 90-day jail sentence. While Fellman's trial was pending, Republican county chairman Edwin "Buzz" Schwenk spoke to me concerning the Fellman cases, wanting to know if Freddie could be given a sentence of probation, permitting him to move to Florida. I told Schwenk in no uncertain terms that in no way would I discuss the Fellman case. I assured him, however, that I would treat Fellman fairly if he were convicted.

Several weeks later, there were discussions concerning a guilty plea by Fellman to satisfy all of his indictments. I agreed to accept the plea, which would be a felony, but made no promise as to the sentence. On May 10, 1971, Fellman took what's called a *Serrano* plea. He did not admit his factual guilt but stated he was pleading guilty to one charge of grand larceny, second degree to avoid prosecution on all the charges, which could have resulted in a much longer prison sentence.

A Suffolk County probation investigator came to me a few weeks later, saying he wanted me to know what Fellman had told him during his interview. He said Freddie had informed him, "that he was not going to jail because he had the goods on all Suffolk County judges and knew what each had paid for their judgeship." Fellman's sentencing came on July 12, 1971. Knowing what he had said to the investigator, I invited Freddie to tell me anything he wished concerning the crime or other matters. I was somewhat baiting him, but he would not speak. I imposed a three-year prison sentence, and he was immediately put in handcuffs and transported to Sing Sing later that day.

Soon after arriving in prison, Fellman got in touch with the U.S. Attorney's office in Brooklyn and told them that Joseph Pfingst, who had been elected to the Supreme Court in 1968, had paid him $50,000 in cash for the nomination. Claiming knowledge of other matters involving Suffolk County politicians, he said he would cooperate in any investigation. He was moved from Sing Sing to the Bergen (New Jersey) County jail so the FBI could bring him back and forth to Brooklyn for the investigation and the trial of Pfingst (in 1972, a federal jury found Pfingst not guilty, though he was convicted on other fraud charges).

Along with New York Mets players Ed Kranepool and Ron Swoboda, Fellman had owned an Amityville, N.Y. bar and restaurant called The Dugout, and he had both players come to the jail to talk and show game movies to his fellow inmates. When Fellman came up for parole after about a year and a half, the warden of the Bergen County jail, a Mets fan, gave him a glowing report. Fellman's celebrated his release at The Dugout.

Fellman appealed my sentence, which was affirmed by the Appellate Division. Serigano also appealed, and his 90-day sentence was modified to an unconditional discharge. Sometime later, I spoke to the presiding justice, Frank Gulotta, about the Serigano ruling, and he told me, "Tom, Serigano was just a poor schmoe for Fellman. We affirmed Fellman's sentence, didn't we?" *Newsday* won a Pulitzer Prize for public service in 1970 for the "Suffolk scandals" investigation. Years later, the paper reported that Fellman came to the party celebrating the win, telling attendees they could not have done it without him.

While the murder trials covered in this book may have been Judge Stark's most horrific cases, none attracted as much worldwide press attention at the time as the 1964 trial of four young men accused of wrecking a Southampton, New York, beachfront home after a party honoring debutante Fernanda Wanamaker Wetherill. Between September 1963 and September 1964, the New York Times *ran no fewer than twenty-six stories about the party, the outrage, the indictments, and the eventual trial, with many reports, including news of the verdict on April 16, 1964, running on page 1 of the paper. Stark was a County Court judge and just beginning his judicial career when he was assigned this nonjury trial and thrust into the national limelight. Here's what he later wrote about this case.*

THE SCANDALOUS SOCIALITES

The Southampton Beach House Revels
September 1, 1963

During my six years on the County Court, I presided over 172 criminal jury trials and disposed of hundreds of cases by guilty pleas. Some trials were covered by the news media, but most were obscure, with few people attending. Perhaps the most widely reported trial was the notorious Southampton house-wrecking case in 1964. Fernanda Wanamaker Wetherill, a seventeen-year-old girl from Philadelphia, celebrated her debut over Labor Day weekend 1963 at Westerly, her parents' Southampton home, with eight hundred guests attending the coming-out party. Many college-age men were invited to the August 31 party, and the debutante's stepfather had rented a thirty-room oceanfront mansion called Ladd House to house them for the entire weekend. The family had hired a band and provided ample liquor for what would become an all-night saturnalia.

After the party at the parents' home was over in the early hours of September 1, the young people went to the oceanfront house to continue celebrating. Events turned into chaos as drunken men and women danced on the mantel (it cracked), swung from the chandelier (it fell to the floor), threw furniture about, and broke nearly every window in the house. Many couples slept on the beach, and by morning the place was in shambles.

The local police learned of the event and investigated. Upon finding out that Donald Leas Jr., the debutante's stepfather, would cover the damages, no further police proceedings were taken, and the incident remained barely noticed by the press. Several weeks later, *Life* magazine learned of the incident and, realizing the story to be made of it, published a prominent article describing the debutante's party and its aftermath as fun and games for spoiled rich children. The headline read "Young people's don't-give-a damn attitude hits a new extreme." The hand-wringing tone extended to the *New York Times*, which in September ran a story headlined "Affluent Delinquency."

The coverage put the Suffolk County district attorney in the national spotlight, and a strong clamor was made to prosecute the youths involved. The district attorney responded with a lengthy indictment charging thirteen men and one woman with malicious mischief, a misdemeanor carrying a maximum one-year jail sentence. The indictment was barebones, giving no details of the specific acts by each participant. Those sixteen, seventeen, and eighteen years of age were eligible for youthful offender treatment, and their cases were severed and disposed of and the records sealed. The other youths, nineteen and over, demanded bills of particulars stating exactly what mischief was done by each defendant. In response, the district attorney specified the mischievous conduct allegedly committed by each youth. This required proof at trial that a defendant intentionally damaged the particular item specified in the bill of particulars.

Eventually, after a number of cases had been disposed of, four defendants remained to be tried together before me without a jury. On arriving at the courthouse on the morning of the trial, I learned there were reporters and photographers present from the Philadelphia and New York City papers. However, photographs had to be taken on the top of the steps outside the courthouse entrance. None could be taken inside the hallways or the courtroom. I refused to be interviewed and photographed in my chambers before starting the trial.

Assistant District Attorney Theodore Jaffe was the prosecutor, and each young man was represented by a prominent criminal trial lawyer. The district attorney had given immunity to several who testified as to what they saw happen. It was very difficult for these witnesses to identify a particular defendant and describe his conduct, being limited, of course, to the particular mischief specified in each defendant's bill of particulars. After all the proof was completed over three days of testimony, I found each defendant not guilty, the prosecution having failed to show me beyond a reasonable doubt that each defendant intentionally damaged the particular item contained in his bill of particulars.

The news of my verdict was widespread, being reported in the Philadelphia and New York City newspapers by individual reporters attending the trial, and reported by the Associated Press and United Press International to newspapers throughout the country, all of which published articles concerning the trial and my verdict. The response was immediate and overwhelming. I received hundreds of letters, postcards, and telegrams from all over the nation and even from Europe, decrying my verdict. The following are samples from some of the writings:

A woman from River Forest, Illinois, said, "People are shocked all across the nation by your verdict. The more I think about it, the more incredible and shameful your actions seem."

A lawyer in New York City wrote, "Your decision warrants your immediate removal from the bench. You have violated your oath of office. I am practicing over 30 years and this is the worst judicial conduct I have ever seen."

An "Irate American" in Buffalo, New York, said, "Judges like you are one of the worst enemies our country has. You encourage juvenile delinquency by your actions, instead of doing the job you are responsible for. Who greased your palm, Judge?"

A woman from South Dakota said, "I am glad I am not a citizen of a state where morals and ethics are so low."

A man writing on a postcard from Herb McCarthy's restaurant in Southampton said, "How much did the blue bloods pay you?"

Someone in New York City wrote, "You will not have to work again when you receive your payoff. The citizens of our country will need gas masks to keep out the smell of this decision."

And last, but not least, a "US citizen and voter" in Golden, Colorado, told me, "Your decision, in my humble thinking, is an insult to human intelligence. It entitles you to worst Judge award for the year 1964. I fervently hope that your decision will make you a political failure and a judicial nothing."

Judge Stark went on to have a nearly four-decade career on the bench. He won election to the New York State Supreme Court twice, acted as supervising judge of the Superior Criminal Courts of Suffolk County from 1978 to 1992, and served as an Associate Justice of the Appellate Term, Ninth and Tenth Judicial Districts from 1985 to 1998. As vice chairman of the Criminal Jury Instructions Committee of the New York State Office of Court Administration from 1972 to 1992, he helped draft uniform jury instructions for the state. In 1984, he was named Judge of the Year by the Suffolk County Criminal Bar Association. Still, the Amityville trial followed him for the rest of his career. He predicted that the first line of his obituary would be "judge who presided over the Amityville Horror trial has passed away." And he was correct.

SOURCES

BOOKS AND TELEVISION PROGRAMS

Anson, Jay. *The Amityville Horror: A True Story*. Engelwood Cliffs, N.J.: Prentice-Hall, Inc., 1977.

Berry-Dee, Christopher, producer. *Deadly Minds*. Aired in 1994 on the Learning Channel.

Gaines, Steven. *Philistines at the Hedgerow: Passion and Property in the Hamptons*. New York, N.Y.: Little Brown & Co., 1988.

Geed, Doug, reporter. Interview of Ronald DeFeo Jr. Aired on News12 Long Island in June 1992.

Holzer, Hans. *Murder in Amityville*. New York, N.Y.: Belmont Tower Publications, 1979.

Kaplan, Stephen and Roxanne Saleh Kaplan. *The Amityville Horror Conspiracy*. Laceyville, Penn.: Belfry Book, a Division of Toad Hall, Inc., 1995.

Osuna, Ric. *The Night the DeFeos Died: Reinvestigating the Amityville Murders*. Nevada: Noble Kai Media, 2003.

Sullivan, Gerard, and Harvey Aronson. *High Hopes: The Amityville Murders*. New York: Coward, McCann, and Geoghegan, 1981.

Teale-Edwards Productions, Inc. *First Person Killers: Ronald DeFeo*. Aired on April 24, 2006, on the A&E Network.

COURT RECORDS

Transcript of Ronald DeFeo hearings and trial

New York State appeals by Ronald DeFeo, Sebastian Ventimiglio, Mario Russo, Anthony Cisco and Daniel Gallagher, including briefs of counsel (DeFeo case) and decisions in all cases

Federal court appeals by Ronald DeFeo, including briefs and memoranda of counsel and decisions

New York State Supreme Court, Ulster County records: divorce action *DeFeo v. Gates*

New York State Board of Parole decisions

ADDITIONAL BACKGROUND MATERIAL

Bench notebooks of Justice Thomas M. Stark and retained copies of jury instruction outlines, presentence investigation reports, psychiatric reports, judicial hearings decisions, and various affidavits

Archives of the *Daily News*, *Life* magazine, *Newsday*, the *New York Post*, *The New York Times*, and *People* magazine

Former Ronald DeFeo websites "The Night Exposed" and "The Injustices of Amityville"